W9-BIR-720

THE GOLDEN
MEAN

THE GOLDEN MEAN

MEAN

Mathematics and the Fine Arts

CHARLES F. LINN

Doubleday & Company, Inc.

Garden City, New York

ISBN: 0-385-04110-1 Trade
0-385-09257-1 Prebound
Library of Congress Catalog Card Number 73–15480
Copyright © 1974 by Charles F. Linn
All Rights Reserved
Printed in the United States of America
First Edition

This last one is for
Nancy

It is easier to believe what you see than
what you hear; but if you both see and hear, then
you can understand more readily and retain
more lastingly; I wish, therefore, so to
arrange my work that everything may be understood
as easily as possible.

ALBRECHT DÜRER / *Instruction in Measurement*

1. Rutherford Boyd experimented for many years with mathematically generated art forms. This one is a Lissajous pattern, formed by an arrangement of pendulums. (Rutherford Boyd photo, from SCRIPTA MATHEMATICA, and with the permission of the Rutherford Boyd Estate.)

The chief forms of beauty
are
order and
symmetry
and
precision
which
the mathematical sciences demonstrate
in a special degree

ARISTOTLE

2. "Liberation," by contemporary artist M. C. Escher, who has been called "the mathematicians' artist." (With permission of the Escher Association.)

A mathematician is a maker of patterns. . . .
His patterns, like the painter's or the
poet's, must be beautiful; the ideas, like the
colors or the words, must fit together in a
harmonious way. Beauty is the final test.
There is no permanent place in the world for
ugly mathematics.

G. H. HARDY

CONTENTS

3. Rutherford Boyd began with parabolas, distorted them, and then rotated the configuration around a center of symmetry. (Rutherford Boyd photo, from SCRIPTA MATHEMATICA, and with the permission of the Rutherford Boyd Estate.)

PREFACE

Euclid alone has looked on Beauty bare
Let all who prate of Beauty hold their peace.

EDNA ST. VINCENT MILLAY

The Pope's emissary stood waiting for the artist's sample to take back with him to Rome. It was to be judged against samples from other painters, so that the Pope could decide whom he would commission to undertake the great project he had in mind. Paolo Uccello had forgotten all about this until that moment, so engrossed was he in his other work. But, with the appearance of great self-assurance, he took up a small brush, dipped it in red paint, and made a quick inscription on a piece of parchment. This he handed to the waiting courtier.

"But it's merely a circle," murmured that gentleman.

"A circle . . . yes," replied Uccello, "but hardly a 'mere circle.' That is my sample."

Apparently the Pope shared Uccello's vision, for he commissioned this fifteenth-century painter to do the work he had in mind. You are certainly entitled to suspect, though, that Uccello may have had other factors working for him—or that Giorgio Vasari, the sixteenth-century art historian, may have embellished the tale.

You would agree, I suspect, that this red circle is, at best, the "Beauty bare" that the poet talks about. Its mathematical properties, though hardly obvious, are generally acknowledged. You multiply the diameter by pi; you draw tangents and secants. You even write appropriate equations. But beauty? The circle as art? This may be something else. Interpretation is needed—but interpretation is the essence of all art. Imagination is essential.

I propose to write a little here about this relationship between mathematics and the fine arts—as I see them. More importantly, I am attempting to present graphic evidence to support my arguments. You must bring to this project your imagination and willingness to interpret.

You will see in these illustrations things which I do not see. Possibly, I will be able to offer interpretations which you have overlooked. And if the result of this experiment can be some enhanced feeling, on both our parts, for the interrelationship of mathematics and the arts, we can count it a successful undertaking.

David Eugene Smith, the great American historian of mathematics, wrote that "The history of mathematics is the history of civilization." If no one has said the same about the history of the fine arts, it is only because this is too obvious.

I have the audacity, then, to propose to examine, in these few pages, the history of civilization from two not distinct points of view. I hope, though, to provoke an argument whenever possible. This is an arguable subject. When two authorities say exactly opposite things, I'll report them and even include some really far-out (to me, anyway) notions.

For the realm of the imagination is a strange and wonderful place, indeed.

So much, then, for what I propose to try to do in this book. What will you do?

Marshall McLuhan has pronounced books "obsolete." If this is true, without qualification, you might as well close this book now and turn on television.

But it seems to me that the obsolete books are those in which the author tries to expound the whole subject—to inflict upon you his interpretations and his ideas. You get so involved in trying to figure out what he is saying (or so in awe of how wise he seems to be) that you never really get involved with the subject matter

4. "Encounter," by M. C. Escher. (With permission of the Escher Association.)

or get a chance to develop your own ideas. Thus, you miss the real fun.

Hopefully, you will get involved here in the business of mathematics and the fine arts through the illustrations, some experimentation, arguing with the theories. That is up to you.

CHARLES F. LINN
Turkey Hill, Connecticut

THE GOLDEN
MEAN

The Mathematical Heart of the Matter

There appeared once, in a mathematical journal, a photograph of a drawing of a rhinoceros by an artist in prehistory. This effort was described, in the caption, as having "significant mathematical characteristics." As such, this example should serve as a reasonable beginning to a consideration of mathematics and the fine arts.

However, I must confess, that while I recognized the picture as that of a rhinoceros, I found the "significant mathematical characteristics" less than obvious. Hence, I could not, in honesty, dramatize the example here.

I cite this example by way of acknowledging my own limitations in the matter of mathematical illusions, and allusions, in art and by way of warning you that you can expect no great subtlety here. I will confine my observations to a relatively few mathematical properties and refer to some rather obvious examples. You take it from there.

The first of these properties, or qualities, is symmetry. Symmetry means balance—but balance of a special kind. Side views of rhinos apart, many of primitive man's inspirations for drawings must have come from nature—such phenomena as starfish, butterflies, and evergreens are symmetrical. In each case you can imagine a line through the center that divides the object into two parts which are mirror images.

Or, close enough to mirror images to satisfy, and inspire, the prehistoric artist.

In fact, a head-on view of a rhinoceros affords an example of symmetry, though, I suspect, it might have a disquieting effect on the potential artist. Indeed, a head-on view of a human is symmetrical. (And I don't want to get involved in a discussion of whether or not the average person has one ear lower than the other.)

In addition to mirror-image symmetry there is "point symmetry," not quite so obvious in nature and art, but a matter for consideration nonetheless. You can find some obvious examples in the letters *S* and *N* and *Z*—or in the sine curve, of which mathematicians are very fond.

Even more difficult to define is the general idea of balance, which, in an artistic sense, means you don't overload one part of a painting—or a building—or a musical composition. I will give mathematical examples here:

. . . the seesaw (lever and fulcrum, if you will),

. . . an equation,

and a Japanese flower arrangement.

You must admit that Uccello's circle qualifies in terms of symmetry-balance.

The word "proportion" is familiar, in the mathematical sense, to everyone who has worked his way through about sixth-grade arithmetic. It is even part of the New Math. Proportion means, for example, that

$$3 \text{ is to } 5 \text{ as } 6 \text{ is to } 10$$
$$\tfrac{3}{5} = \tfrac{6}{10}.$$

The application of proportion in the arts is just about the same. In particular, when drawing or sculpting the human body, the artist will have the length of the head as a certain fractional part of the length of the torso. And, the ratio of torso length to total body length should be about a certain number.

The idea of proportion is very important in music, the ratio of frequencies—string lengths—is basic to the whole description and categorization of sound. This does not lend itself readily to pictures, but does merit consideration later.

On the other hand, artists have deliberately varied the proportions in order to produce a particular distortion or grotesque effect. It seems to me that the very act of distorting—assuming a calculated distortion—reflects a mathematical influence.

These first two math-art qualities, symmetry and proportion, are applied in several areas—painting, sculpture, music, architecture. A third, the idea of space perception, applies just to paintings and, to an extent, architecture.

If you look out on a playground or athletic field, you take for granted that people appear smaller when they are farther away from you. If you draw a picture of this scene and try to make it look realistic, you will make some of your people appear substantially smaller than others. That is, you deliberately distort in order that the picture will look "right." The amount of distortion will affect the impression of the picture on your viewer, and thus you are involved in a mathematical consideration.

Cavemen artists generally (from what little evidence we have) did not worry much about the matter of space perception.

A study in perspective by Jan Vredeman de Vries, sixteenth-century Netherlands artist. Vredeman was a principal messenger of the new art style throughout Germany, Scandinavia, and the British Isles. (With permission of Dover Publications.)

But then they probably were not overly concerned about realism.

In fact, artistic works through the first thirteen or fourteen centuries of the Christian Era appear flat. Most of the paintings are on religious themes, and the artists obviously were much more concerned about the message than about depth perception, mathematically figured or otherwise.

Very recently, Grandma Moses, whose paintings were described as "primitive," made quite an impact, despite the fact that her cows, trees, houses, and all often appear to be the same distance from the viewer.

Drawings by small children also reflect their artists' lack of concern for space perception. More than that, small children are inclined to draw railroad tracks parallel.

"Certainly," you will argue, "for they are parallel."

Granted. But if you look down a stretch of track, the two rails appear to draw closer together at some distance from you.

(Look out for the train!)

This means that if you are going to have your pictures of a railroad appear realistic, you must introduce a distortion. To conjure up the most realistic impression possible, you must have just the right degree of distortion. And you must be consistent about it. Here, mathematics can help.

The painters who studied this problem—perspective—in the thirteenth, fourteenth, fifteenth, and sixteenth centuries, were mathematicians of sorts (whether or not they would have admitted it). Incidentally, Uccello was one of the early experimenters in perspective. Their studies became a basis for a new mathematical study, projective geometry.

"Mathematics," for me, means "patterns." The study of mathematics involves the search for patterns, the extension of patterns, and generalizations on patterns.

These patterns range from very simple number sequences,

$$2, \quad 4, \quad 6, \quad 8, \quad 10, \quad 12 \ldots$$

through some slightly more complicated, such as

$$1, \quad 1, \quad 2, \quad 3, \quad 5, \quad 8, \quad 13, \quad 21,$$

5. "The Brooklyn Bridge: Variation on an Old Theme," by Joseph Stella. (Collection of the Whitney Museum of American Art, New York.)

to the more sophisticated patterns of groups, rings, even algebras, geometries, and topologies.

I wish I had as handy a definition of art.

I think it safe to say, however, that much art—painting, mosaics, architecture, music, tapestry, stained-glass windows—involves patterns and, as such, may be thought of as an area of application of mathematics.

(I don't really mean to limit "art" to those forms just mentioned. They are convenient examples. "Art" must mean any manifestation of creativity. Poetry should be included. As such, mathematics itself is an art. In fact, mathematicians are inclined to exalt over the "beauty" of a proof.)

Having tried to build up the idea of patterns and regularity, I'll inject a contradictory note. Total absence of pattern—randomness —may be considered a mathematical property. In fact, mathematicians work hard to prepare tables of "random digits" in which there is no regularity or repetition in the way the digits occur.

The decimal expansion of the number pi is thought to be an example of randomness:

$$3.141592. \ldots$$

To admit this notion to the agenda here would complicate the problem impossibly. So I propose to say no more about it, other than to note that there seems to be a direct analog in the carefully planned, apparently random drawings of some paintings.

Having mentioned some of these more esoteric manifestations of the relationship between mathematics and the fine arts, I propose now to move to a possibly more mundane example—the Pythagorean theory of music.

The beautiful in sound must depend upon a succession
of notes related to each other and a prime by the
simplest possible ratios.

PYTHAGORAS / (Sixth century before the Christan Era).

The perfect fifth is the simplest mathematical
ratio and therefore the closest relation that
exists between two different tones. For this
reason the perfect fifth . . . must constitute
the basis of the whole system of tone combinations.

From a twentieth-century text on
the theory and practice of tone-relations.

Music by the Easy Numbers

Having for some years argued that fractions should be abolished, and, having argued particularly strongly about multiplication and division of fractions, I am a bit chagrined at having to use fractions—even multiplying and dividing them—in talking about the Pythagoreans and their music, theory, and practice.

Be of good cheer, however. The Pythagoreans were convinced that all relationships in the physical world could be expressed in terms of simple ratios. (Musical notes were among these physical phenomena, though, as you will see, a bit of number juggling was needed to "conserve" the "simple ratios.")

And, with or without the New Math, you can eliminate the division and do all of it with multiplication of fractions. (That is, you need not worry about "inverse operations" or "inverting divisors.")

The basic discovery of the Pythagoreans was this:

The notes produced by two strings of equal diameter and tension will vary according to the lengths of the strings.

This is a fact of our particular physical world. While much has happened in music since the time of the Pythagoreans, this relationship remains.

In particular, they noted that if one string were half as long as another, they would give the same tone, though that from the shorter string would be higher. This is the relationship called *the octave*.

(If you don't know anything about music, or even if you know a little, you may find it helpful to try out some of these simple ideas on a piano. I'll keep the discussion easy. Promise!)

In particular, I would recommend sticking with the key of C. (Just find middle C and count up and down.)

That is, the ratio of string lengths for an octave is

$$1 : 2.$$

Given any string length with its note, halve the length and you raise the pitch by an octave. Double the length and you lower the pitch by an octave.

The 1:2 ratio worked out so nicely, how about the 1:3—the next simplest ratio? The ratio is smaller than for the octave, so you can expect to get a higher pitch. It is, in fact, that which is called the *fifth*. The combination of the basic tone and its fifth is a particularly pleasant or, at least, inoffensive one. (Many people would probably describe the effect as insipid, but the Pythagoreans were much pleased.)

The "fifth" is actually that 1:3 ratio dropped down an octave. That is, the string length is doubled, and the ratio becomes 2:3. In the key of C, this corresponds to the G.

Lengthen the string by half—over that which gives C—and you decrease the pitch by a fifth. That is, the ratio is 3:2. The note corresponds to low F. Make that string half as long, raise the pitch an octave, and you have F, with a ratio of 3:4.

$$C=1$$
$$1 \cdot \tfrac{3}{2}=\text{low F}$$
$$\tfrac{3}{2} \cdot \tfrac{1}{2}=\tfrac{3}{4}\text{—f}$$

The four notes—C, F, G, c—were the basis of very ancient Greek music, really more declamation than music. They are said to form the range of the legendary lyre of Orpheus.

The Pythagoreans were much intrigued by the interval of the fifth and developed their entire scale by advancing the pitch by fifths. Going a fifth above G, they had d. Its ratio was

$$1 \cdot \tfrac{2}{3} \cdot \tfrac{2}{3} \cdot 2=\tfrac{8}{9}$$
$$\text{fifth} \quad \text{fifth} \quad \text{octave}$$

Up another fifth

$$\tfrac{8}{9} \cdot \tfrac{2}{3} = \tfrac{16}{27}$$

—the ratio associated with A.

The Pythagoreans then had

C	D		F	G	A		c
$\tfrac{1}{1}$	$\tfrac{8}{9}$		$\tfrac{3}{4}$	$\tfrac{2}{3}$	$\tfrac{16}{27}$		$\tfrac{1}{2}$

If you go up another fifth from A,

$$\tfrac{16}{27} \cdot \tfrac{2}{3} = \tfrac{32}{81},$$

and drop this an octave,

$$\tfrac{32}{81} \cdot \tfrac{2}{1} = \tfrac{64}{81},$$

you'll have a note to fill one of the gaps. (The gaps are more obvious here because of my lettering. The Pythagoreans found the musical pitch gap just as obvious.)

Up another fifth from E,

$$\tfrac{64}{81} \cdot \tfrac{2}{3} = \tfrac{128}{243},$$

which filled the last gap. The scale, called "diatonic," looked like this:

C	D	E	F	G	A	B	c
$\tfrac{1}{1}$	$\tfrac{8}{9}$	$\tfrac{64}{81}$	$\tfrac{3}{4}$	$\tfrac{2}{3}$	$\tfrac{16}{27}$	$\tfrac{128}{243}$	$\tfrac{1}{2}$

The Pythagoreans saw some mathematical disadvantages to this arrangement.

First, such ratios as

$$\tfrac{64}{81}, \quad \tfrac{16}{27}, \quad \tfrac{128}{243}$$

could hardly be classed as "simple." (Now, if you were going to juggle ratios a bit in order to eliminate these non-simple varieties, how would you go about it?)

Second, a succession of the 8:9 ratios, which they called *tones,* did not produce an octave. In fact, six tones give

$$(\tfrac{8}{9})^6 = \tfrac{262144}{531441}$$

which is not equal to ½. The difference between this and an octave they called a *comma*.

Third, the notes on the scale were not evenly spaced. In fact, the steps from note to note on the scale went like this:

$$C \quad D \quad E \qquad F \quad G \quad A \quad B \qquad c$$
$$\tfrac{8}{9} \quad \tfrac{8}{9} \quad \tfrac{243}{256} \quad \tfrac{8}{9} \quad \tfrac{8}{9} \quad \tfrac{8}{9} \quad \tfrac{243}{256}$$

(If you look again at the piano keyboard, you'll notice a correspondence with this sequence of intervals. There is a black key between each two white keys which are separated by an $\frac{8}{9}$ ratio.)

Anyway, later Pythagoreans proposed that the interval of the "major third"—that is, from c to E—be $\frac{4}{5}$ instead of $\frac{64}{81}$. This may seem to be a bending of the physical facts to suit a mathematical theory, but the ancients were not above this, and, anyway, it was so close. The ratio of the "major sixth"—from C to A, for example—would become $\frac{3}{5}$. (A is an octave above the fifth below E—

$$\text{fifth below E} \qquad \tfrac{4}{5} \cdot \tfrac{3}{2} = \tfrac{6}{5}$$
$$\text{octave above this} \qquad \tfrac{6}{5} \cdot \tfrac{1}{2} = \tfrac{3}{5}.)$$

Then they had

$$C \quad D \quad E \quad F \quad G \quad A \quad B \quad c$$
$$\tfrac{1}{1} \quad \tfrac{8}{9} \quad \tfrac{4}{5} \quad \tfrac{3}{4} \quad \tfrac{2}{3} \quad \tfrac{3}{5} \quad \tfrac{8}{15} \quad \tfrac{1}{2}$$

and, if they continued to have B one tone above A, B's ratio became 8:15.

Of course, the intervals between notes still are not all the same. And, there remains a comma. For, if you were to begin at C and tune up four fifths

$$C \longrightarrow G \longrightarrow D \longrightarrow A \longrightarrow E$$

or, up two octaves and a third,

$$C \longrightarrow C \longrightarrow C \longrightarrow E,$$

you would expect to arrive at the same note. But, by the numbers, you get in the first place

$$\tfrac{2}{3} \cdot \tfrac{2}{3} \cdot \tfrac{2}{3} \cdot \tfrac{2}{3} = \tfrac{16}{81}$$

and, in the second

$$\tfrac{1}{2} \cdot \tfrac{1}{2} \cdot \tfrac{4}{5} = \tfrac{1}{5}.$$

That is, the comma was $^{16}\!/_{81} / \tfrac{1}{5}$.

Some years later, Arixtoxenus apparently proposed that this comma be distributed over the intervals, giving what has become known as the equal-tempered scale.

Many of the Greek mathematicians wrote treatises on music. Fragments of those by Euclid and Ptolemy have survived, but most were lost in the turbulent centuries following the collapse, first of law and order in Alexandria, and then of Rome itself. The Pythagorean music theory was preserved through the writings of Boethius, whose textbook was the principal source for the study of music at such universities as Oxford and Cambridge down to the seventeenth century.

However, for much of this time, music was studied, not as a basis for singing or playing an instrument, but rather in terms of the mathematics of the subject and the mystical properties of numbers—à la Pythagoras.

In beauty, as I said, the effect is previous to any knowledge of the use; but to judge of proportion we must know the end for which any work is designed.

EDMUND BURKE / *A Philosophical Enquiry into the Origin of Our Ideas of the Sublime and the Beautiful*

For beauty there are three requirements: First, a certain wholeness or perfection, for whatever is incomplete is, so far, ugly; second, a due proportion or harmony; and third, clarity, so that brightly colored things are called beautiful.

THOMAS AQUINAS

There are some who will by no means allow of this, and say that men are guided by a variety of opinions in their judgment of beauty and of buildings; and that the forms of structure must vary according to every man's particular taste and fancy, and not be tied to any rules of art. A common thing with the ignorant, to despise what they do not understand.

LEON BATTISTA ALBERTI

Proportions, Divine and Otherwise

There are several questions, more or less related:

1. If you are constructing a building, particularly a public building, such as the Greeks thought so well of, what ratio do you give to, say

height : width

in order that it have a "most pleasing" appearance?

2. What relationship should there be of the parts to the whole, inside and outside, so that these parts—entrance ways, towers, rooms—will seem to "be the right size"?

3. What ratios do you use among head, torso, legs, total height, so that your paintings or sculptures of the human form will appear "true to life"?

4. A historical question: Did the Greeks and the Egyptians, in particular, have some formula to guide them in designing buildings and, possibly, sculpture?

A natural reaction, I suspect, to this list of questions, is to dispose first of number 3. Why not just measure a lot of people, find some kind of average, and use these numbers in your design? This is quite appropriate in the statistic-oriented twentieth century. In fact, the approach seems a sensible, and obvious, one for any era.

But, the problem of the right proportions—and a nice formula—has intrigued artists and art historians, at least since the revival in the West of interest in and knowledge of the Greeks—about the twelfth century. "The Greeks," so the argument runs, "had such a nice thing going for them in the simple ratios in music. They must have applied the same principle—or, at least, tried to apply the same principle—to architecture and sculpture."

And, "true" proportions do not look right in paintings, for example, where you are trying to represent three-dimensional figures in a two-dimensional space—the canvas.

A really complicating matter has been, historically, a mathematical one. The Pythagoreans discovered irrational numbers. That is, they found that there are natural geometric relationships which cannot be expressed in terms of the ratio of one whole number to another.

This brings me to question 4 of my list and prompts a bit of a mathematical digression.

But, before I expound, try a small experiment. On the opposite page are several artist's drawings of a Greek-type temple.

1. Which has, to you, the "most pleasing appearance"?
2. Between the top one and the bottom one, which has the more pleasing appearance?
3. Of the two middle ones, which do you prefer?
4. Of the top two, which do you prefer?

Now, on with the mathematical digression—and the mathematics is not very complicated. So, don't tune me out.

Legend has it that the Pythagoreans first noticed that the ratio of the diagonal of a square to a side cannot be expressed in terms of whole numbers. That is, if you let the length of the side be 1 unit, the length of the diagonal is $\sqrt{2}$ units. To construct this with straightedge and compass, as Plato specified, is a very simple matter. But, the ratio of

$$\sqrt{2} : 1$$

just can't be expressed in terms of whole numbers.

The Pythagoreans, so the story goes, were badly shaken by this discovery. In fact, it is said that they drowned one of their members who let out the secret.

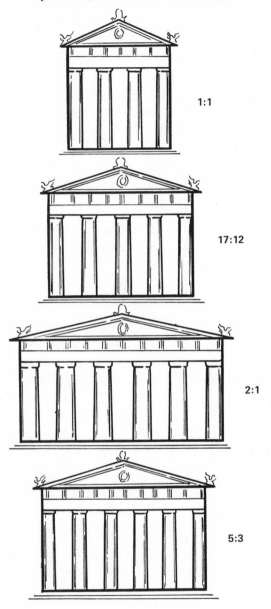

Greek temples. (Nancy Linn.)

The ratio which really stirred the argument in art circles, also involving an "irrational" number,—and the argument continues to the present—comes from an item in Euclid's *Elements:* ". . . to divide a line segment such that the ratio of the large part to the whole is equal to the ratio of the small part to the large part."

This means that if the small part is thought of as a unit, the large part is $\dfrac{1+\sqrt{5}}{2}$ units long. This ratio,

$$\frac{1+\sqrt{5}}{2} : 1,$$

cannot be expressed as the ratio of one whole number to another.

Again, the geometric construction is rather easy. But, the numerical relationship is no go.

"And thereby," as they say, "hangs a tale"—of much argument —and the spinning of some very surprising theories over the years.

Later—much later—scholars began to call this special division of a line segment the "golden section," and the rectangle formed by the two parts, "the golden rectangle." As people began to find, or think they had found, ways in which this ratio,

$$\frac{1+\sqrt{5}}{2} : 1,$$

had been used by the Greeks, and even the Egyptians, in their sculpture and architecture, they became even more enthusiastic and called it the "divine proportion."

The argument is that the proportions of the "golden rectangle" are the most pleasing to the eye, and, furthermore, the Greek temples and the pyramids were constructed to afford this aesthetic appeal.

Did your opinions of "the most pleasing" temple design support the "divine proportion" theory?

I have tried this experiment with groups of people and, rather surprisingly to me, the golden-section design seems to come out

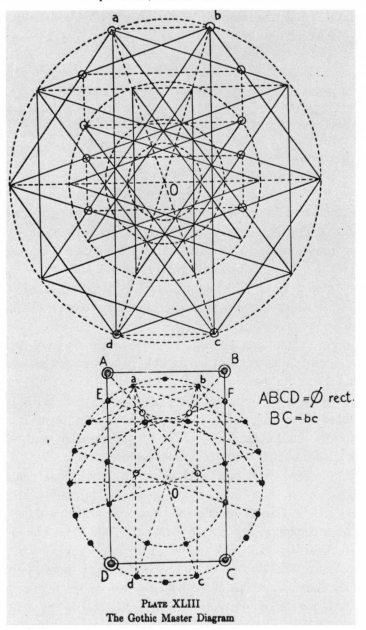

ABCD = ϕ rect.

BC = bc

PLATE XLIII
The Gothic Master Diagram

6. This has been called "the Gothic master diagram" since it is found in one or another form in much Gothic architecture. You will note the appearances of the "golden section ratio."

ahead. Of course, the bottom sketch gives a good approximation to the "golden rectangle."

That is

$$\frac{1+\sqrt{5}}{2} \text{ (often called "}\phi\text{")} \approx .618,$$

so $5:3$ or $.6$

is not far off.

In fact, in the sequence,

$$2, \quad 3, \quad 5, \quad 8, \quad 13, \quad 21, \quad 34,$$

where each term is the sum of the two before it, each succeeding pair of numbers gives you an improved approximation to the "divine proportion." (This is called the "Fibonacci" sequence. I mention the name only because I must refer to it later.)

The "golden rectangle" has the property that if you cut off a square that which remains is another "golden rectangle." That is, there is an area relationship involved.

This observation has prompted the invention of some strange and wonderful theories, with remarkable geometric designs accompanying them. I'm not enthusiastic enough about these claims to allot them space here (but check the Bibliography, particularly those titles listed under "Hambidge" in the Appendix). On the other hand, I can hardly "knock" the theories. Too often, important, and useful, results have come from strange notions about numbers.

This question about the Greek ideas on proportions could be settled so nicely if only we could go to the primary sources—writings of the Greeks themselves. But, practically nothing survived on architecture and human form. Pliny the Elder hinted that the Greek artists had settled on "proper proportions" for their human figure. The writings of those pagan Greeks fared poorly in the early Christian centuries, and their notes on the human form must have been particularly displeasing. The ideal forms were undoubtedly related to Apollo, Athena, and other pagan deities.

Dürer pointed out, much later, that the ideal forms of Apollo and Athena were easily translated into ideal forms of Jesus and Mary. But earlier Christians were not that broad-minded. No one rescued and preserved this part of Greek art as Boethius did for music. (Boethius, incidentally, seems to have been impressed by the arguments of Vitruvius on proportion.)

And now, the "golden section" enthusiast, attempting to recapture the Greek technique, shows the human form with the ø ratio much in evidence.

Leonardo and Dürer, on the other hand, regarded the question of proper proportions for human figures as requiring experimentation. Dürer, in particular, gathered statistics on the human form, as a basis for a beginning figure. He then varied the figure according to a system of proportional increase and decrease until he produced figures too slim and too stout. Some of these were very strange, and Dürer warned against their misuse.

(Dürer's work on the human figure was well thought of, even among his contemporaries. Francisco Pacheco, a painter of the Spanish Inquisition, recommended that the female figure should be studied from Dürer's drawings rather than from living models.)

What you really have are two theories—two mathematical theories, if you will—proportion, particularly in architecture.

(A geometric theory: Proportions for actual construction are laid out with compass and straightedge—even a carpenter's square. Which may have been what Christopher Wren was inclined to call "natural beauty."

(An analytic or arithmetic theory: Proper numerical proportions are established one way or another—and, then you measure.

Even the strongest supporters (Hambidge, for example) of the geometric theory concede that this is not an efficient method of planning construction. There is, however, support for the practicality of the theory. Some of the most dramatic evidence comes from the notes and sketches of Villard de Honnecourt, dating to about 1250.

These were made during the period of the construction of many Gothic cathedrals. Villard showed, first, how the Gothic arches were laid out.

7, 8. Two sketches by Christopher Wren, the English architect, who was considered by his contemporary Sir Isaac Newton to be the greatest geometer of the time. (Courtesy of THE ARCHITECTURAL RECORD.)

Then he turned to the problem of cutting the keystone, which was based on a right triangle of proportions $1 : \sqrt{3} : 2 \cdot \sqrt{2}$.

And there you are right back at the irrational numbers, though one commentator, in what has to be tongue-in-cheek, says, "The ordinary mason did not, in fact, have to know he was dealing with an irrational number."

Villard showed an elaborate scheme for getting this proportion —-involving a spiral formed by arcs of increasing size, which the master mason actually laid out with compasses.

(Several such spirals are preserved on stone in the Chartres Cathedral, and Villard may have learned the technique there. Dürer, incidentally, used the spiral in reverse.)

So, apparently, the geometric approach has merit, though, once again, there is little direct evidence from this period. The Gothic renaissance died with the Black Death, and remaining manuscripts fared little better with the "humanists" of the fifteenth and sixteenth centuries than did the Greek writings with the early Christians.

There have been a variety of analytic theories of proportion.

One authority asserts that "In dividing a horizontal line, the golden section is decidedly less pleasant than bisection. In dividing a vertical figure . . . the golden section is less pleasant than the ratio $1:2$."

The French architect, Corbusier, used a $3:5$ ratio in his design of the "ideal house," though he paid lip service to the "divine proportion" by inscribing it over his elevation drawing. Corbusier also used 144 subdivisions of a six-foot man as the basis for drawing the human figure.

"Ah, hah"—the divine proportion enthusiast will point out— "144 is a number in the Fibonacci sequence!"

Some translators say that Vitruvius argued that the proportions of a temple ought to be those of a well-formed human figure. He divided the height of a man into 96 parts. Cardan used 180 parts.

(You'll notice that all three of these numbers have many factors. For example, 180 has factors of 2, 3, 4, 5, 6, 9, 10, 12, 15, 18, and so on. Then ⅑, ¹⁄₁₀, ¹⁄₁₂ . . . of the total figure come out to be even numbers of parts.)

You can find an authority to support almost any theory you have in mind. If this multiplicity of authority-with-mathematics suggests confusion, that is precisely what came—"chaos" is a better description—at least for architectural theory.

Out of this chaos came some early nineteenth-century observations which, while hardly mathematical, have real common-sense appeal.

Lord Kames (Henry Home) in *Elements of Criticism* (1839):

> I need go no further for a proof than the very room I occupy at present; for every step I take varies to me, in appearance, the proportion of length to breadth; at that rate, I should not be happy but in one precise spot, where the proportion appears agreeable.

Archibald Alison, *On Taste* (1811):

> . . . when any improvement . . . is made in the construction of the forms of art, so that different proportions of parts are introduced, and produce their end better than the former, the new proportions gradually become beautiful, while the former lose their beauty.

Perhaps there is nothing mathematical about "proper proportions," after all.

Not by Math Alone
. . . An Egyptian Interlude

Some years ago—before Nasser made the scene—if you were to mention "Egypt," I would most likely think "pyramids." This was not, I suspect, an unusual reaction.

The pyramids, while certainly not the most imaginative architectural works in the world (or, even in Egypt), must still be considered among the most impressive. The ancients rated them as one of the Seven Wonders. And a modern tourist would still be awed by their size, even if he didn't stop to think about the problems of building them 6,500 years ago.

The mathematical shape must appeal to even the most down-to-earth person. If he has a little imagination (and imagination is certainly a requisite for the creative math-type too), he will think about the mathematical reputation of the Egyptians—and, maybe, about Egyptian mysticism (possibly reading some of the ancient manuscripts)—even visit the pyramids, and begin to suspect that there may be more of mathematical importance there than the shape.

A table of data might be a good place to look for such mathematical relationships in this ancient architecture:

Place	Base (")	Height (")	Angle
Medum	5,682	3,619	51°52′
Gizeh (Khufu)	9,068	5,776	51°52′
Gizeh (Khafra)	8,475	5,664	53°10′
Gizeh (Menkaura)	4,154	2,581	51°10′

Place	*Base ($''$)*	*Height ($''$)*	*Angle*
Dahshur (South)	7,459	4,134	$\left\{ \begin{array}{c} 43°\ 5' \\ 55°\ 1' \end{array} \right\}$
Dahshur (small)	2,064	2,034	44°34'

Looking over these figures, you must be struck by the fact that while sizes of the pyramids vary considerably, most of the "angles" are of about 51–53 degrees. That is, the ratio of the heights to the base lengths of the pyramids is about the same.

If you work out these ratios, you'll find something like the following:

Medum	1.57
Gizeh (Khufu)	1.57
Gizeh (Khafra)	1.5
Gizeh (M)	1.609
Dahshur (S)	1.8
Dahshur (s)	≈ 1

The pattern shows up better here. Most of the ratios are close to 1.6. Compare that to the 1.618 ratio for the "divine proportion" and you have evidence for a claim that the Egyptians also were committed to the idea of one proportion being more pleasing than any other.

Or, so the argument goes, anyway.

While this theory of pyramid design gives a nice example of mathematics in architecture, you really should take a hard look at it. If the Egyptian builders had really wanted a 1.618 ratio of base to height, don't you think they could have had it?—not 1.57, 1.8, 1.5, or even 1.609.

They were able to construct one of the largest pyramids so that the difference in length between the longest and shortest sides of the base was less than eight inches. That is, the percentage of error was less than .1 per cent.

The same pyramid was evidently supposed to be oriented according to the four cardinal directions. The average error here was about three minutes (a minute being $\frac{1}{60}$ of a degree).

Viewing the argument in that light, I find the evidence a bit weak for "divine proportion" theory. If the builders could devise methods for getting these accuracies—and other ingenious methods, such as their method for leveling the base of a building—I suspect they could have done better by the base-to-height ratio, if they had wanted to.

Another mathematical argument goes like this: The height corresponds to the radius of a circle, the circumference of which is equal to the perimeter of the pyramid at ground level.

This works rather nicely for the pyramids at Medum and the larger one at Gizeh, but accuracy tapers off in others. This theory, though, led some people to the idea that a very accurate value of pi was built into the pyramids.

Actually, the proportions of the pyramids have nothing to do with mathematics. But, you must know a bit about Egyptian religion and mythology. The Sun-god figured prominently in their beliefs, and the Pharaoh, when he died, was thought to join the Sun-god in his daily romp across the sky. Thus, the tomb of the Pharoah was to be a staircase to some celestial chariot stop.

As such, the pyramid was a practical compromise on a conical structure (there's an example in Heliopolis) which was the symbol of the Sun-god. The cone represented rays of the sun shining on the earth, and the angle of the pyramid, so the argument runs, was an approximation of the sun's rays.

An ancient manuscript notes that:

Heaven has strengthened for thee the rays of the sun in order that thou mayest lift thyself to heaven as the eye of Re [the Sun-god].

One student of these matters reports:

These great triangles forming the sides of the pyramids seem to fall from the sky like the beams of the sun when its disk, though veiled by storm, pierces the clouds and lets down to earth a ladder of rays.

Now, I must admit that this explanation made more sense to me than the divine-proportion business. But I thought to check the argument when next I saw the sun piercing the clouds and letting down to the earth a ladder of rays. Alas, though I observed on several occasions, the angle seemed always to be much greater than 55°—steepest of the large pyramids.

Of course, these could have been off days.

My point being that 'tis easy to overdo such a business as the analysis of the relationship of mathematics to the fine arts, particularly if the focus of your analysis is not around to defend himself. You can expect, also, that the analysis may see a steady progress toward a goal they themselves deem desirable.

The white rhinoceros picture, drawn by a prehistoric artist, was described by the mathematics journal as showing "significant mathematical characteristics." If indeed it does, these properties must be related to the problem of showing solid figures on a plane surface. That is, the artist wanted the rhino to look "real"—"true to life."

This may seem a highly desirable goal, and you might expect to trace improvements in techniques through the years. Early Egyptian painting shows such improvements, but later efforts show no depth perception—perspective, if you will—at all. This does not necessarily represent a lapse, or loss of technique, on the part of the later artists. That is, artists did not work steadily at solving this problem of how to represent three-dimensions on two, from the unknown drawer of the white rhinoceros until the final solution by the artist-mathematicians of the fourteenth, fifteenth, and sixteenth centuries. In certain periods, artists abandoned attempts to deal with the space problem—art as a reflection of reality. One such switch came about in Egypt. This probably was just a change in attitude of the artists, and there have been such changes in the last fifty years. For the Egyptian artist, there were at least two alternatives:

Tell a story.

Pure design.

The latter, in particular, has mathematical implications. In fact, the Egyptians made use of quite an important mathematical idea in their designs, though they did not formally state the idea.

(The Egyptians used many important geometric ideas without

stating them formally. Greek mathematicians adopted many of these ideas and developed them in purely mathematical form. Consequently, the Greeks have become known as the mathematicians, while, frequently, the long centuries of trial and error work, and practical application, by the Egyptians, are overlooked. But, that is another story.)

Anyway, this mathematical idea which shows up in Egyptian art design was also used extensively, but much later, by the Moslems. They conquered Egypt in the seventh century of the Christian Era, and then swept over much of the Mediterranean region, adapting and improving upon local techniques wherever they went. Thus, the techniques in ornament and design have come to be related to the Moslems.

The mathematical description of the idea was not developed formally until 1924.

I propose, then, to talk a little about the mathematical implications of these two problems in art—perspective and ornament—in the next two sections.

Painting is the most astounding sorceress. She can persuade us through the most evident falsehoods that she is pure truth.

JEAN-ETIENNE LIOTARD

The aim of the architect is to make his work harmonize with the demands of the senses and to devise methods for deceiving the eye, as far as possible; his object being not actual, but apparent, symmetry and eurythmy.

HELIODORUS OF LARISSA

Systematic and Proper Deception

As you may have noticed, I've tried to choose contradictory quotes with which to begin sections. This is in keeping with my announced intention to offer authoritative support for almost any point of view that you may want to consider. That I have not presented contradictory observations here is not due to lack of

A Vredeman study in perspective, with multiple "vanishing points." (With permission of Dover Publications.)

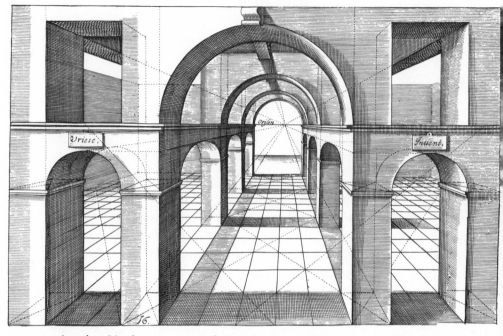

Another Vredeman perspective study. You might compare this with one of the Escher drawings. (With permission of Dover Publications.)

remarks, by prominent citizens, to the effect that works of art should not attempt to portray "Truth" or "Reality."

In fact, I suspect, most artists these days would say just that.

And many architects would argue that a building should be, first of all, functional—useful.

The two quotations do, however, point up two varieties of distortions or deceptions which artists and architects have practiced, one of which has already lent itself to systematic analysis, and one which may do so in the future.

So, let me ask, in good mathematical form, that

if you want to show in a painting what something really looks like,

then, what techniques must you use?

(Mathematics, in more serious circles, consists of *if* . . . , *then*'s. This is merely an aside and has nothing to do with the relationship of mathematics to art. However, I might point out that if you prefer to reject the hypothesis, then obviously what follows has no meaning. It is the same in mathematics and a lot of other matters.)

To dramatize these two problems of deception, I'll call one "mathematical" and the other "anti-mathematical."

One problem is that of representing a three-dimensional scene —that which you see—on a two-dimensional space—the canvas.

That is, you want to give the impression of depth where there is no depth.

You want to give the impression that one object is farther away than another, though they are really the same distance from the person looking at your painting.

You want to give the impression of volume where there is only area.

You want, in short, to deceive, but in such a way that your drawing is "acceptable." Because if you didn't deceive, your drawing would not "look right." Again, let me emphasize that assumption —*If* you want the scene to look "true to life."

This general problem of systematic deception concerned artists from prehistoric times to the thirteenth, fourteenth, and fifteenth centuries, when it was finally worked out.

If two objects are actually the same size, then the one farthest away will appear smaller—but how much smaller?

A human, or animal, figure facing you in the drawing will have different proportions from those of a view from another angle—or of a sculpture—assuming, of course, that you have resolved to your satisfaction the problem of proper proportions—but by how much are the proportions changed?

Lines which actually are parallel do not appear parallel in the drawing. But if they aren't to be drawn parallel, how should they be drawn in order that they look "right"?

The angles of a building—in particular, right angles—generally don't have a proper appearance if they are shown as right angles. But if not right angles, then what kind of angles will give the proper appearance?

Vredeman studies in perspective. (With permission of Dover Publications.)

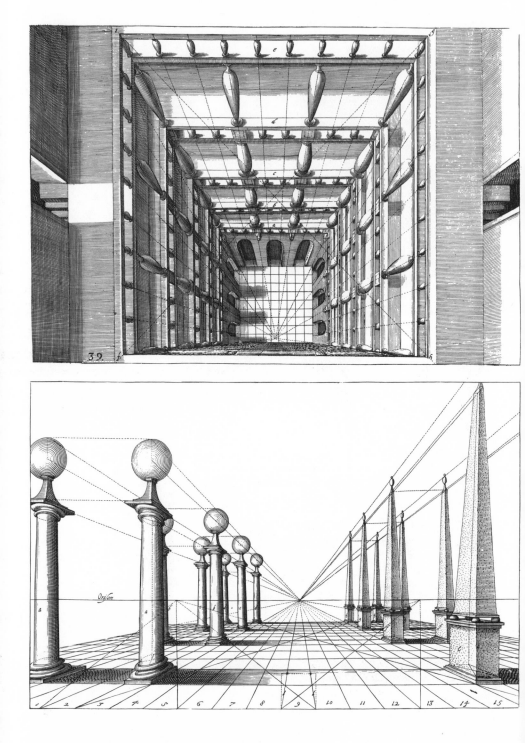

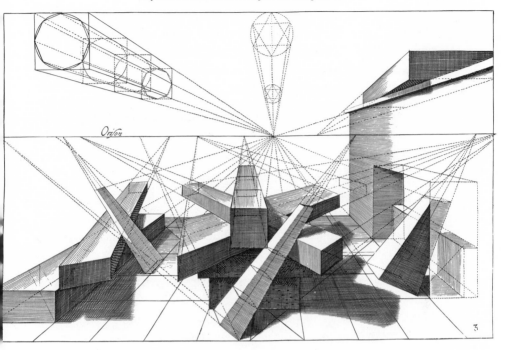

Artists categorize these questions as matters of *perspective*.

The over-all problem can be approached in two ways, the one suggested by the railroad/telegraph-pole photo, where the "parallel lines" recede toward a point. (I think first of perspective in terms of railroads, which is why this particular photograph has always intrigued me. Who knows? Perhaps the problem of perspective would have been sooner resolved if the artists had had railroads and telegraph poles to study.)

Dürer wrote a treatise on perspective, as did Piero della Francesca. The notebooks of Leonardo da Vinci are sprinkled with observations on the subject.

Perspective therefore is to be preferred to all the formularies and systems of the schoolmen, for in its province the complex beam of light is made to show the stages of its development wherein is found the glory not only of mathematical but all of physical science, adorned as it is with the flowers of both.

Perspective is nothing else than the seeing of an object behind a sheet of glass, smooth and quite transparent, on the surface of which all the things may be marked that are behind this glass; these things approach the point of the eye in pyramids, and these pyramids are cut by the said glass.

A second object as far removed from the first as the first is from the eye will appear half the size of the first, although they are of the same size.

There are three divisions of perspective as employed in painting. Of these the first relates to the diminution in the volume of opaque bodies; the second treats of the diminution and disappearance of the outlines of these opaque bodies; the third is their diminution and loss of color when at a great distance.

Perspective employs in distances two opposite pyramids, one of which has its apex in the eye and its base as far away as the horizon. The other has the base toward the eye and the apex on the horizon. But the first is concerned with the universe, embracing all the mass of the objects that pass before the eye, as though a vast landscape were seen through a small hole, the number of the objects seen through such a hole being so much the greater in proportion as the objects are more remote from the eye; and thus the base is formed on the horizon and the apex in the eye, as I have said above.

The second pyramid has to do with a peculiarity of landscape, in showing itself so much smaller in proportion as it recedes farther from the eye; and this second instance of perspective springs from the first.

Apparently, some overdid the study of perspective—at least, others thought they did. Vasari began his biographical sketch of Paolo Uccello with:

Paolo Uccello would have been the most gracious and fanciful genius that was ever devoted to the art of painting, from Giotto's day to our own, if he had labored as much at figures and animals as he labored and lost time over the details of perspective;

for although these are ingenious and beautiful, yet if a man pursues them beyond measure he does nothing but waste his time, exhaust his powers, fill his mind with difficulties, and often transforms its fertility and readiness into sterility and constraint, and renders his manner, by attending more to these details than to figures, dry and angular, which all comes from a wish to examine things too minutely; not to mention that very often he becomes solitary, eccentric, melancholy, and poor as did Paolo Uccello. This man, endowed by nature with a penetrating and subtle mind, knew no other delight than to investigate certain difficult, nay, impossible problems of perspective, which, although they were fanciful and beautiful, yet hindered him so greatly in the painting of figures, that the older he grew the worse he did them.

Poor old Paolo. I can't help but wonder what Vasari would have to say about some of the efforts of Maurits C. Escher.

Jan Vredeman de Vries, who was a contemporary of Vasari and thus did not qualify for Vasari's *Lives,* summed up the development of perspective in a remarkable book published in 1604. Some of Vredeman's plates appear throughout this section, without comment, for I thought it appropriate to follow Vredeman's own remark, in the introduction to his book, that he did not want to be tiresome or tedious to his readers but would let his illustrations speak for themselves. Vredeman, incidentally, acknowledges a debt to Dürer in the study of perspective.

Vredeman (the "de Vries" means "the Frisian" or "Frieslander") gave a guide of five components of perspective:

1. The base line that defines the level on which the imaginary viewer or painter stands.
2. The perpendicular lines that frame the whole system.
3. The horizon—whatever is above the horizon cannot be seen from above; whatever is below the horizon cannot be seen from below.
4. The parallel lines, or lines of foreshortening, that converge at the "eye point" or central vanishing point.

5. The diagonal or oblique lines that converge at distance points or secondary vanishing points.

Vredeman also states that, throughout his book, he assumes the viewpoint of a man five and a half feet tall. The man, by the way, appears in one of the illustrations here.

Very little is known about Vredeman, but apparently he did not become solitary, eccentric, melancholy, and poor through his study of perspective.

When questions on perspective were finally answered systematically—and, as you can see, artists worked at this over a period of some thousands of years—there was a substantial mathematical by-product; in fact, a new kind of geometry—a geometry in which parallel lines meet, and you can't really talk about perpendicular lines, or the measuring of angles. This geometry is called "projective" by the mathematician. Now, for the anti-mathematical "deception":

Perhaps the attentive eye will glance along the various sides and note that there is not a single mathematically straight line on the entire building. At first we shall be inclined to take for granted inaccurate measurements, or the effect of earthquakes or some similar cause. But, whoever stands opposite the right-hand angle of the front side, so that the upper cornice of the flank can be sighted in a foreshortened line, will discover an outward bend of several inches, which can only have been produced by intention. And more things of the same kind will be found. These are expressions of the same feeling which called for the outward curving of the columns, and which everywhere sought to give apparently mathematical forms the pulsation of a living organism.

Nineteenth-century art historian
JACOB BURCKHARDT / about the temple of Poseidon.

The Greeks . . . had the feeling, which was encouraged by their high culture, and their happy climate, that straight lines have a cramped and stiff effect. They saw that Nature avoids the rectilinear and develops its most attractive forms in swelling curves, and so they endeavored to make the construction of their buildings resemble Nature, to transfer to them the beautifully curving forms which surrounded them, and thus to infuse the lifeless forms of art with a breath of living Nature.

JOSEPH HOFFER, / another nineteenth-century art historian.

These refinements, designed to relieve the monotony of mathematical regularity and give to these buildings a "pulsation of life," were subtle devices indeed. Let me cite a few numbers.

In the Parthenon, for example,

there is an upward curve on the cornice of four inches in about 228 feet on one face; and of 2.75 inches in 100 feet on another face; all columns lean inward toward the sides of the building— the extent of the lean is about 1 : 150; angle columns lean inward diagonally; side walls lean inward, to the extent of about 1 : 80; doorjambs lean slightly toward one another—about 1.5 inches in 33 feet; the pediment leans forward.

Photographs don't show these refinements. You must, I suspect, see for yourself, and then you will probably need to align and measure carefully.

Incidentally, the description "refinements," which I obviously like, was applied by William H. Goodyear, who made a very extensive and careful study of these phenomena. He also used the term "symmetrophobia," though he says he did not invent it.

The effects cannot be dismissed as "inaccuracies in construction" or as due to settling of the buildings. The curves and leanings are too regular.

And once these devices were noticed and measured in the mid-nineteenth century, it was found that Vitruvius gave instructions for their construction. He suggests, for example, a 1:40 forward inclination of the pediment. I should add, however, that scholars seem to be able to find, in one or another translation or version of Vitruvius, support for almost any architectural theory. (In this instance, the interpretation appears justified.)

There are examples of Greek temples, which have no "refinements."

1. The temple at Aegina
2. The temple of Nike Apteros, on the Acropolis
3. The temple of Phigalia in Arcadia
4. The Erechtheum, on the Acropolis

A possible reason for their appearance in some temples and not in others is neither mathematical nor artistic. Construction with these refinements simply was much more expensive than without. Thus, the Parthenon, which was built at the height of Athens' "Golden Age," shows the most refining, while the Erechtheum, built during the Peloponnesian War, has none. (And the leaders probably made much ado about wartime austerity.)

Scholars who first noticed these curves and leanings suggested that they were meant to compensate for what amount to optical illusions—*apparent* saggings, *apparent* fanning effects of columns, *apparent* backward leaning of the pediment.

Later observers, including Professor Goodyear, were inclined to talk in almost mystical terms—"a feeling of life, inspired the whole building, dispelling its mathematical rigidity," "pulsation of a living organism," "pyramidal appearance so essential to the idea of repose and strength."

These are difficult points to counter effectively, but I will give one example and leave you to experience the Parthenon and, say, the Lincoln Memorial, and draw your own conclusions.

(Nancy Linn.)

Is the base line here curved or straight?

To my (perhaps prejudiced) eye, it appears to sag a bit—and since this is a schematic of the pediment-cornice arrangement of the front of the temples, where the Greeks applied a bit of upward curvature, I'm inclined to support the compensation of illusion argument. More supporting evidence comes from the use of certain kinds of refinements in Italian cathedrals.

You can observe some architectural deceptions more easily in many of these cathedrals—variations in size and shape of the arches, the subtle curves, and sloping floors. The last device, incidentally, is used on stages to give the effect of greater depth. In some cathedrals the nave is narrower away from the main entrance. Again, the effect is apparent increased depth.

The cloisters of several cathedrals have subtle curves which are much like those of the second temple court at Medinet Habou in Egypt. The Egyptians, incidentally, used the sloping-floor effect.

The knowledge of these devices probably was preserved by the Byzantines during the period from 300 to 1000, or so, when the architecture business was a little slow in the West. You can find refinements used in St. Sophia's, in Istanbul, for example.

The architects apparently knew what they were doing, for, though some of these variations are substantial, they aren't noticed by the casual (or even the enthusiastic) tourist. In fact, Professor Goodyear, who made the rounds just to study these "refinements," said that he missed them at times on his first inspection and didn't really notice them until he had made careful measurements.

So, photographs don't show much, though he brought back some nice ones.

"All very interesting," said a friend to whom I had expounded this wisdom. "But it's hardly mathematics—just some people trying out architectural tricks, some of which seem to work pretty well."

He seemed to be hinting that I was stretching things to include the discussion under the heading of "mathematics and the arts." I now have a two-point rebuttal, the better of which, fortunately, I came up with on the spur of the moment, and thus did not leave him entirely in command of the debate.

First, if these refinements are intended to "break the monotony of mathematical regularity," they deserve consideration here. Isn't anti-math closer to math than is non-math?

9. The bend in the plan of the choir of the Siena Cathedral shows rather clearly in this photo. (W. H. Goodyear photo, with permission of THE ARCHITECTURAL RECORD.)

10. Church of Sant' Apollinare Nuovo at Ravenna, Italy. The original building dates to the sixth century, though it was reconstructed in the ninth century and later. (W. H. Goodyear photo, with permission of THE ARCHITECTURAL RECORD.)

More importantly, it may be that we just haven't invented powerful enough, or subtle enough, mathematics to cover these refinements. Much mathematics has come out of the efforts of people in one or another field just trying out ideas and devices.

Artists played around with perspective for literally thousands of years before the techniques were systematized, scientifically and/or mathematically.

Artists from the early Egyptians through the Moslems experimented with design forms in tilings, mosaics, and other ornament and apparently knew that their variety was limited. But it was not until 1924 that Georges Polya, using the recently invented group theory, proved that there are just seventeen different kinds of designs, all of which had been used by the ancients.

So, perhaps, the mathematics of the "refinements" is still to be invented.

In contemplating the surviving relics of any period in which the soul of a people achieved aesthetic utterance through the arts of space, it is clear that in their architecture and in their ornament they had a form language as distinctive and adequate as any spoken language.

CLAUDE BRAGDON

Symmetry signifies rest and binding, asymmetry, motion and loosening, the one order and law, the other arbitrariness and accident, the one formal rigidity and constraint, the other, life, play and freedom.

DAGOBERT FREY

Symmetry, Patterns, and Ornament

Some say that nature is the inspiration for all art. Some say that nature is the inspiration for all mathematics.

The first "some" may not include any of the second "some." That is, in the language of mathematics, the intersection of these two sets may be the null set.

Certainly, you will find artists who quibble about the first suggestion. And mathematicians who quibble about the second. And artists and mathematicians who say that "quibble" is much too mild a word.

But there seems enough evidence to warrant an investigation of these relationships, that is, the triangle of art, nature, and mathematics.

In fact, you have a handy common denominator in the idea of symmetry:

([the symmetry of reflection—mirror images, if you will, in nature's mirrors;

([the symmetry of rotation—exotic creatures and flowers— turn them part way around and they look the same;

([expansion symmetry—toss a pebble in a pool, and the pattern of ripples moves out, alike in shape, but different in size;

([translation symmetry—the figure is repeated, but keeps its direction.

In man's efforts to reflect nature, these symmetries show up most consistently in the repeated designs which, studied together, are called "ornament."

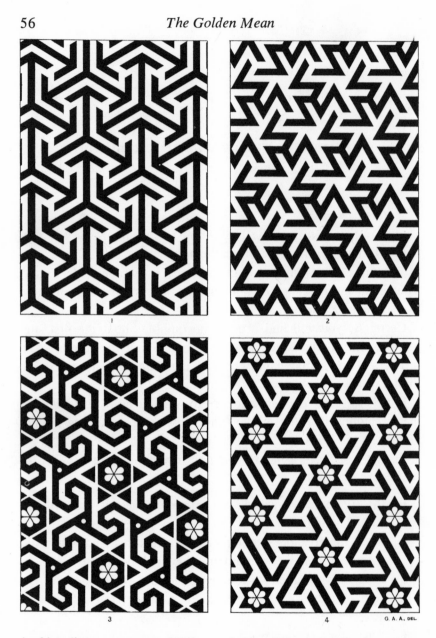

Arabian diaper ornament. (With permission of Dover Publications, from Audsley, DESIGNS AND PATTERNS FROM HISTORIC ORNAMENTS.)

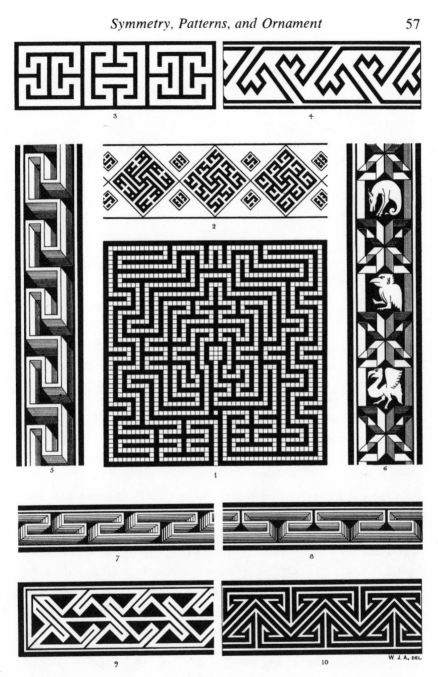

Middle Ages fret ornament. (With permission of Dover Publications.)

Now it may be that artists of our time will object to my calling symmetrical, repeated designs an art form. In which case, they are free to reduce me to an asymmetric polygon in an abstract canvas.

And present-day mathematicians may be unhappy about my suggesting that ornament is mathematics. They are welcome to try to prove, rigorously, that I do not exist.

The evidence is in my favor, however. These symmetrical, repeated designs, often even involving mathematical forms, were created by a variety of peoples.

The Egyptians
Western artists, of the "Middle Age" (and here you even see
    some attempts to show "depth of field")
The Moors
The Arabs

Both the Moors and the Arabs were Moslem people, who were forbidden by their scriptures to use the human form in their art. Thus, repeated patterns, particularly in mosaics, were particularly significant in their art forms. One of the finest examples, or, I should say, sources of examples, is the Alhambra in Spain, where all seventeen varieties of repeated design are found. Of course, the Alhambra long antedates Polya's proof that there are only seventeen possible types.

Polya's examples are free of embellishment. Take a look at a few here, and see if you can relate them to some of the examples from the Alhambra.

You can try your hand at creating variations on these seventeen themes. Or, if you prefer an irrational touch, here is an ornament proposed by E. B. Edwards, who supports the argument that Greek architecture, sculpture, or whatever, was developed around the golden rectangle, the $\sqrt{2}$ rectangle, and such forms.

Here you start with crossed $\sqrt{2}$ rectangles (that is, the ratio, of the length to the width is $\sqrt{2}$: 1. You can construct one of these easily by beginning with a square, drawing in a diagonal, and then using that as a side of your rectangle, with the side of the

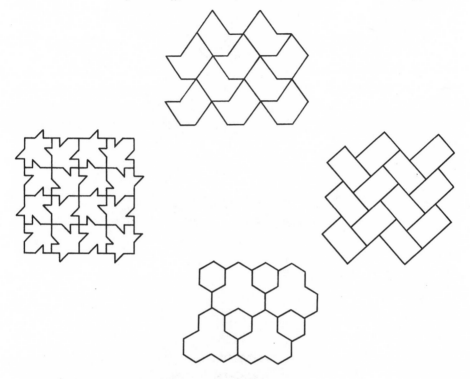

Examples of repeated design. (Nancy Linn.)

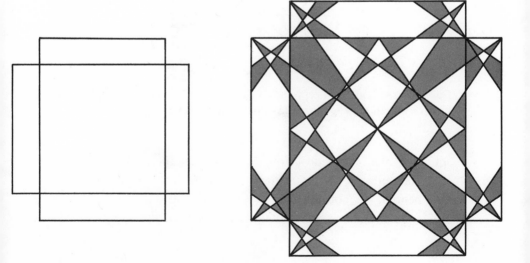

Design from a "root two" rectangle. (Nancy Linn.)

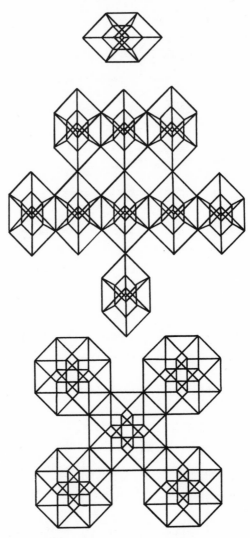

Designs based on an interpretation of the tesseract. (Original ideas proposed by Claude Bragdon. Drawn by Nancy Linn.)

square as the other side). Join vertices to midpoints of sides. Add
those crisscrosses in the corners. Alternate black and white . . .
and, behold, . . . ornament.

Claude Bragdon suggested that ornament of the twentieth cen-

S. R. A. & G W. DEL

Moresque interlaced ornament. (With permission of Dover Publications.)

tury should involve projections of four-dimensional figures. He proposed several examples based on the tesseract, the four-dimensional analog to the cube.

I see no evidence that Mr. Bragdon's proposal (of about 1927) has become a basis for modern ornament. In fact, there seems to be little "modern ornament," as such. There are, however, quite a few examples of "pure" mathematical forms in art, and here you can get into the act yourself.

Of course Beethoven's *Eroica Symphony* or Michelangelo's ceiling of the Sistine Chapel can be reduced to an adequate mathematical formula. There is, however, one little catch. The only person capable of making such an all-inclusive analysis must be able to feel the emotions that Beethoven and Michelangelo felt, to think in sound and paint as they did—in short, to have an imaginative perception of everything that went into those masterpieces. That means that he himself would be equipped both by nature and by training, to be a composer and painter of the first rank. He would, of course, have to be equally gifted and trained as a mathematician. Unfortunately, when such a universal genius comes along again, a second Leonardo da Vinci, he probably will be too much interested in his own original creations for him to bother with making analyses of the masterpieces of the past.

J. MURRAY BARBOUR

Let us examine a crystal. We are at once interested by an equality between sides and between the angles of one of its faces; the equality of the sides pleases us; that of the angles doubles the pleasure. On bringing to view a second face in all respects similar to the first, this pleasure seems to be squared; on bringing to view a third it appears to be cubed, and so on. I have no doubt, indeed, that the delight experienced, if measurable, would be found to have exact mathematical relations such as I suggest; that is to say, as far as a certain point, beyond which there would be a decrease in similar relations.

EDGAR ALLAN POE

The Measure of Beauty

The question of measuring beauty—that is objective assessment beyond "Very nice," "Exquisite," "This appeals to me"—has troubled scholars and other laymen at least from the time of the Greeks. And, beginning with the Greek philosophers, there has been wide disagreement.

Plato, who proposed to exclude poets from his Republic, and who considered a work of art as merely an imitation of the actual object which was, in turn, a mere shadow of his "ideal," contended that "If arithmetic, mensuration, and weighing be taken away from any art, that which remains will be little indeed."

Plotinus, on the other hand, argued that "Beauty is rather a light that plays over the symmetry of things than the symmetry itself, and in this consists its charm."

Aristotle supported the Platonic view. "The main elements of beauty are order, symmetry, definite limitation, and these are the chief properties that the mathematical sciences draw attention to."

There you have probably the extreme positions on the question of beauty, in particular, beauty in art—on the one hand, the analytic view; on the other hand, a mystical description. In between these extremes are arguments for evaluating art in terms of the pleasure you experience. Here's Helmholtz again: "The more easily we perceive the order which characterizes the objects contemplated, the more simple and more perfect will they appear, and the more easily and joyfully shall we acknowledge them. But an order which costs trouble to discover, although it will indeed also please us, will associate with that pleasure a certain degree of weariness and sadness."

Between the time of Aristotle and that of Helmholtz, a great variety of scholars made a great variety of comments on the question of the measurement of beauty. (Presumably Man-in-the-Street [and Woman-in-the-Street] voiced correspondingly varied opinions, but these were seldom recorded and we are stuck with the view of scholars.)

The mathematicians Descartes, Euler, and Sylvester made their views known. The philosophers philosophized—Edmund Burke, in the eighteenth century; likewise Frans Hemsterhuis ("The beautiful is that which gives the greatest number of ideas in the shortest space of time"); Kant and Spencer in the nineteenth century.

The poets got their words in. The quote at the beginning of this section comes from Edgar Allan Poe's "The Rationale of Verse." In another essay, "The Philosophy of Composition," Poe analyzed, step by step, the construction of *The Raven,* thus putting the creation of a work of art on a systematic basis.

And so, as you can see, there was a great deal said on the matter of beauty and how you might measure it. But, apart from some rather limited efforts by Poe and Sylvester, no one did much about developing a general systematic approach until George David Birkhoff wrote his *Aesthetic Measure,* well into the present century.

Birkhoff was one of the great American mathematicians who, among other accomplishments, coauthored (in 1932) the first geometry textbook that was really different from that of Euclid. Birkhoff was the first to acknowledge the hazards in trying to establish a mathematical basis for the measurement of beauty— and you may disagree violently (though, of course, in a philosophic way) with what he has done. But his effort is, I believe, worth serious consideration.

No one, least of all Birkhoff, would claim anything approaching infallibility for his system. His discussion is sprinkled with "in my opinion[s]," and he notes at one point that "Even when the class [of objets d'art] is sufficiently restricted, the preference of different individuals will vary according to their taste and aesthetic experience. Moreover, the preference of an individual will change somewhat from time to time."

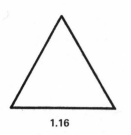

1.16

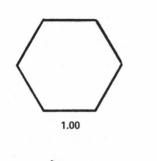

1.00

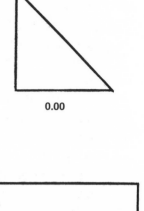

0.00

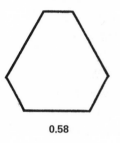

0.58

0.62

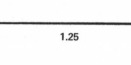

1.25

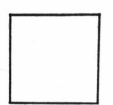

1.50

−0.11

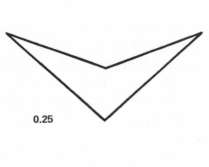

0.62

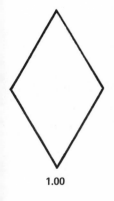

1.00

0.25

0.50

(Nancy Linn.)

To appreciate the hazards of this undertaking, you really should get involved. Consider the set of polygons—polygonal forms, if you will. Which has the greatest aesthetic appeal? Can you rate them, relatively at least?

Scattered around the previous page are assorted polygons— among the ninety which Birkhoff evaluated as a first, and least complicated, application of his aesthetic measure formula. Rate these from 1 to 12, then compare your ratings with those under the drawing before going on to a bit of explanation on how Professor Birkhoff arrived at his numbers.

He qualifies these evaluations of polygonal beauty: "When used as an element of composition, in painting, the isosceles triangle may introduce an adventitious element of symmetry. But in the more elementary question of triangular form, per se, the equilateral triangles are superior to the scalene."

That is, the context in which a figure appears affects its aesthetic appeal. For example, the figure

would receive a low rating under the Birkhoff system.

But, when it is repeated, as the basic figure of a pattern, the effect is rather appealing. (See opposite page.)

At least, I think so.

Many Japanese paintings are based on scalene triangles.

And Birkhoff himself said that "irrelevant symmetry is tiresome."

With these reasonably well-modulated (I hope) words of caution in mind, I propose that you consider the Birkhoff criteria for polygons (keeping in mind that this is the very simplest example of the applications of his thesis).

The basic formula is

$$M=O/C;$$

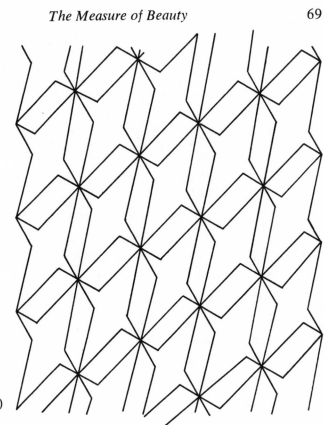

(Nancy Linn.)

that is,

$$\text{aesthetic measure} = \frac{\text{order}}{\text{complexity}}.$$

"Order," he says, "depends on five factors:

vertical symmetry	(V)
equilibrium	(E)
rotational symmetry	(R)
relationship to a horizontal-vertical network	(HV)"

and a negative factor, euphemistically called "unsatisfactory form" (F).

Thus,

$$O=V+E+R+HV+F.$$

"Complexity" means the number of indefinitely extended lines which contain all the sides of the polygon.

For the square, then, which Birkhoff rates highest,

V=1   (1 and 0 are the only possibilities)
E=1   (a square at rest, that is)
R=2   (a bit arbitrary, perhaps—but the entire system is largely arbitrary. "Nevertheless," Birkhoff wrote, "it seems to correspond to the facts observed."
HV=2   (The square is the basic component of the most familiar co-ordinate network.)

Thus, the plus factors total 6. There are no "unsatisfactory forms" about the square—very small or very large angle; diversity of niches; small vertex to vertex distances.

Complexity equals 4.

Hence, the measure of the square's aesthetic appeal is

$$\tfrac{6}{4}=1.5.$$

You need not agree with this verdict. I, for example, am inclined to favor the regular hexagon, for which Professor Birkhoff had

V=1   R=3
E=1   HV=1

but, C=6, and

$$M=\tfrac{6}{6}=1.0.$$

The larger angle of the hexagon seems to me more attractive than the 90° angle of the square. If I were to develop a theory of aesthetic measure, I'd give serious thought to rigging it in favor of the regular hexagon.

What is your inclination? Care to back up your choice with a mathematical argument?

Now the systematic point of view which we have adopted does not permit us to take refuge in an obscure similarity between the shape of a vase and that of the human body, nor in an occult quality of living form, nor even in mystical properties of number.

G. D. BIRKHOFF

Professor Birkhoff, incidentally, did not think much of the claims for the "divine proportion."

Mathematical connotations of urns and vases these days seem limited to those rather foolish probability situations: "Now, if 7 white balls and 5 black balls are placed in an urn . . ." Quite a comedown from the discussion in *Aesthetic Measure*. Birkhoff concedes that the vase problem—that is, mathematizing the assessment of a vase's beauty—is very difficult. He suggested considering:

1. points of the contour line where a tangent is vertical;
2. points of inflection—where the curvature changes from convex to concave;
3. the end points of the contour line;
4. "corner points"—where direction of the tangent changes abruptly.

The examples he uses are Chinese vases. Greek vases usually had handles, which, he claims, detract from their beauty. (Could it be that the Greeks, of all people, sacrificed the beauty of lines for utility?)

At this point Professor Birkhoff proved himself to be truly an experimental investigator by devising several vase forms, one of which he rated at 1.08 on his scale—substantially higher than the Chinese vases.

It would be highly absurd to try to formulate a definitive theory of aesthetic measure, valid for the music of the future as well as of the past.

G. D. BIRKHOFF

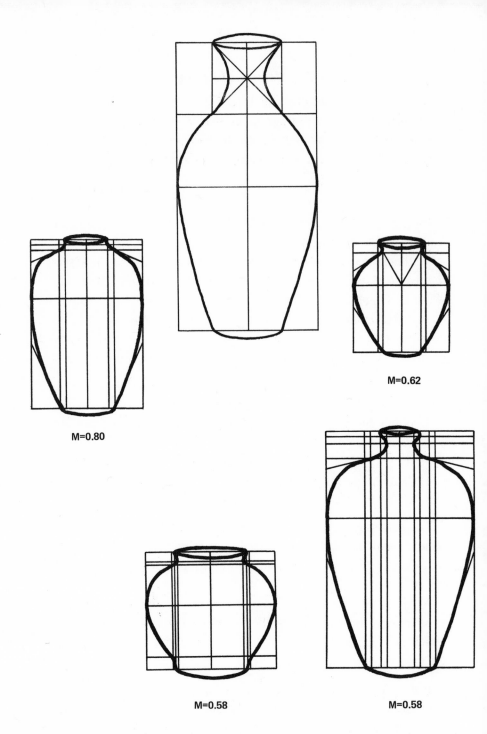

M=0.80

M=0.62

M=0.58

M=0.58

Reconstruction of vase designs used by George David Birkhoff in his mathematical analysis of aesthetics. (Nancy Linn.)

Birkhoff made a thorough study of Western music theory before attempting to apply his measurement standards to chords. I can hardly do justice in a page or so to his effort, but I'll cite an example or two, and, if music is your interest, you can take it from there.

Even if you aren't musical, you can try out a few chords on the piano. No experience needed; you can do it all on the white keys. Just locate C, and away you go.

Birkhoff scores one point if the chord is major, but none if it is minor. Compare the

$$C - E - G$$
or $$F - A - C$$
or $$G - B - D$$

with

$$D - F - A$$
or $$E - G - B$$
or $$A - C - E.$$

(Music theorists work on the basis of four-part harmony— C - E - G - c, for example—and this figures in Birkhoff's theory.)

The triad

$$C - E - G$$

is said to be in "fundamental position," while

$$E - G - C$$
and $$G - C - E$$

are called "inversions." He rates the fundamental position as more pleasing than an inversion, though they are both the same chord.

A point is deducted if the chord contains a dissonance—a minor second, such as

$$E - F \quad \text{or} \quad B - C$$

—a major second, like

$$C - D, \quad D - E, \quad F - G, \quad G - A, \quad \text{or} \quad A - B$$

—or their complements:
a major seventh,

$$C - B \quad or \quad F - e;$$

a minor seventh,

$$D - c, \quad E - d, \quad G - f, \quad A - g, \quad or \quad B - a.$$

Well, you take if from there—to the piano. Compare your evaluations with Birkhoff's.

$$C - E - G \qquad \text{rates a "5."}$$
$$D - F - A \qquad \text{receives a "2."}$$
$$B - D - F \qquad \text{breaks even with a "0."}$$

Of the dominant seventh variations,

$$G - B - D - f \qquad \text{has a "5,"}$$
$$B - D - f - g \qquad \text{is worth only a "2."}$$

Need I say again that this measurement system is highly subjective and arbitrary and all those other things which you might not associate with mathematics? On the other hand, a mathematical system is, basically, arbitrary, if not subjective. You choose your axioms, so long as they don't contradict each other, and build a consistent system on these. Which is precisely what Professor Birkhoff has done.

Modern musicians would disagree, perhaps violently. But, that is quite another problem.

The word "Verse" is used here as the term most convenient for expressing generally, and without pedantry, all that is involved in the consideration of rhythm, rhyme, meter, and versification. . . . the subject is exceedingly simple; one tenth of it, possibly, may be called ethical; nine tenths, however, appertains to the mathematics. . . .

Edgar Allan Poe
"The Rationale of Verse"

I have mentioned Edgar Allan Poe's interest in a mathematical basis for constructing a poem. Birkhoff was similarly concerned, and, while I have not included poetry among the art forms here, you may be interested in his rating of a few examples. (Once again, the modern "word artists" might dismiss the entire business; that also is a different problem.)

Here are Professor Birkhoff's criteria—axioms, if you like:

rhyme;

repetition of vowel sounds;

alliteration (words with the same beginning letter);

musical vowel sounds ("a" as in art; "u" as in tuneful, "o" as in ode);

ease of speaking.

These axioms led him to the following comparative ratings:

> In Xanadu, did Kubla Khan
> A stately pleasure-dome decree:
> Where Alf, the sacred river, ran
> Through caverns measureless to man
>   Down to a sunless sea.

From Coleridge's *Kubla Khan*

—M=.77

> Tell me not, in mournful numbers,
>   Life is but an empty dream!—
> For the soul is dead that slumbers,
>   And things are not what they seem.

From Longfellow's *A Psalm of Life.*

—M=.65.

Birkhoff's own attempt at putting theory into practice brought the following poem, *Vision,* to which he gives a .62:

> Wind and wind the wisps of fire,
> Bits of knowledge, heart's desire;
> Soon with the central ball
> Fiery vision will enthrall.
>
> Wind too long or strip the sphere,
> See the vision disappear!

The first stanza of *The Raven,* which Poe analyzed rather mathematically, received a .75.

> Once upon a midnight dreary,
>   while I pondered, weak and weary,
> Over many a quaint and curious
>   volume of forgotten lore,—
> While I nodded, nearly napping,
>   suddenly there came a tapping,
> As of someone gently rapping,
>   rapping at my chamber door.
> " 'Tis some visitor," I muttered,
>   "tapping at my chamber door:
>
> Only this and nothing more."

. . . music has a more immediate connection with pure sensation than any other of the fine arts, and, consequently . . . the theory of the sensations of hearing is destined to play a much more important part in musical esthetics, than, for example, the theory of perspective in painting.

H. HELMHOLTZ / *Sensations of Tone*

I found another Helmholtz quote which I like very much. It isn't directly related to the problem at hand, that is, not specifically. . . . But, what he says applies, I think, to scientific and particularly mathematical undertakings in general.

So, I'll pass it along here:

I was like a mountaineer who, not knowing his path, must climb slowly and laboriously, if forced to turn back frequently because his way is blocked but discovers, sometimes by deliberation and often by accident, new passages which lead him onward for a distance. Finally, when he reaches his goal, he finds to his embarrassment a royal road which would have permitted him easy access by vehicle if he had been clever enough to find the proper start. In my publication, of course, I did not tell the reader of my erratic course but described for him only the wagon road by which he may now reach the summit without labor.

From his introduction to *Sensations of Tone*

Curves and Pitch

You may recall that a few chapters back, Pythagoras was rather happy with his newly discovered relationship between musical notes and lengths of strings. It was only natural that he should want to extend the range of his string-produced notes beyond the octave mentioned.

But, the Pythagoreans were quite distressed over their discovery that some things in this world cannot be explained in terms of simple ratios. As it turned out, some of the relationships involving strings and musical tones do require what are now called "irrational numbers" for their description.

What Pythagoras had done was to keep the diameter of the strings and the tension on them the same . . . and vary the length. This produced different musical sounds. Suppose,

    a. you keep length and tension the same, but vary the diameter of the string;

    b. you keep length and diameter the same, but vary the tension.

What effects do these conditions have on the sound?

You can probably offer some intuitive impressions—

> heavier strings produce lower notes
> greater tension produces higher notes—

and I'm sure these effects were noted at a very early date. But, precise mathematical descriptions were not given until the middle of the seventeenth century.

These are known as "Mersenne's Laws," after their originator:

I.   (The "law of Pythagoras").
II. When a string and its length remain unchanged, but the tension is varied, the frequency of vibration is proportional to the square root of the tension.
III. For different strings of the same length and tension, the period of vibration is proportional to the square root of the weight of the string.

For example, if you had two strings of the same length and diameter, but with one under double the tension, the vibration frequency of the one would be about 1.4142, etc., times the other. And there is one of those miserable incommensurables that the Pythagoreans were so unhappy about.

Or, if you double the weight of a string, its vibration period is multiplied by that same square root of 2.

Better still, why not quadruple the tension and/or the weight, and you double the frequency and/or period.

I realize I haven't said anything about frequency and period, and I'll get to that shortly. But you can take a look at the wires of a piano and get an idea of what is involved.

The modern piano—more accurately, pianoforte—has a range of 7¼ octaves. To get this range with just the law of Pythagoras, you would have to have the longest string about 150 times the length of the shortest. Such an arrangement would be a bit inconvenient.

So, the wires for the high notes are under greater tension and those for the low notes are heavier. And many people can have pianos in their houses without having to construct rooms half the length of a football field.

For the following experiment you will need some tuning forks, a soft-lead pencil, some tape and paper. The idea is to attach the pencil to a tuning fork; strike the fork and let the pencil translate the vibrations to the paper. To do this—and it's a tricky procedure at best—you must move the paper at a uniform, rapid rate under the steadily held tuning fork.

No task for a person with numerous thumbs, as they say, or unsteady nerves, for the experiment is hard to control. At least you can get the idea that the vibrations of tuning forks may all produce a certain type of curve. If you pull the paper rapidly enough—so you can tell the ups and downs apart—and at a constant speed, you may be able to see that the ups and downs are "evenly spaced."

That is, the translated vibrations of the tuning forks produce a curve such as that shown below—one in which the distance from A to B is the same as the distance from B to C; from C to D, and so on. The heights/depths of the ups and downs seem to decrease as the sound becomes softer, but the "across" distances between corresponding points remain the same.

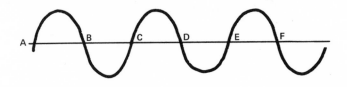

(Nancy Linn.)

For another tuning fork, with the paper moved at the same speed, the space between ups and downs is again constant. But this constant distance is not the same as for the first tuning fork. That is, different tones produce different numbers of waves in a given length of time.

The number of vibrations/waves per given length of time, usually a second, is called the *frequency* of the sound. Frequency is associated with the "pitch" of a note. The time required for one vibration/wave is called its period. (And now you may want to reconsider Mersenne's Laws.) Each musical sound has its own frequency and, thus, will produce its own unique curve. You can get at an analysis of musical sounds through the examination of these curve-signatures. (In fact, if you have access to a cathode-ray oscilloscope, you can get very good results from the experiment —no pencils or paper needed. Just take along some tuning forks.)

One numerical way to compare notes is through comparison of their frequencies. For example, "high c"—an octave above "middle c"—has a frequency twice that of middle c. (The ratio of string lengths is 1 : 2, of course.) First, though, you need a standard for comparisons of pitch or frequency, just as you need standards for comparing distances, or weights. For one or another reason, the pitches of other notes have been figured from that of *a*. But what frequency should be assigned to *a?*

In the eighteenth century, there was no standard for *a,* and its pitch varied from the 393 of the organ at the Strasbourg Cathedral to 567—the "church pitch" of northern Germany.

To say the very least, a composition played at these various churches would sound dramatically different. It was not until 1939 that, at an international conference, the pitch of *a* was standardized at 440.

However, before relating the pitches of other notes to this standard *a,* I must remark on the resolution of a problem of long standing: the distribution of a comma.

It's a problem that undoubtedly did not concern Pythagoras's wife, but did bother him—and musicians for hundreds of years. It came from his scale of notes, and although the comma shows up in smaller intervals, the most convenient explanation is this:

If you begin at a c, and count up 12 fifths, you will reach another c, seven octaves above the first. Since the frequency ratio of the fifth is $\frac{3}{2}$, the frequency ratio of 12 fifths is

$$(\tfrac{3}{2})^{12} \approx 129.75.$$

But, the frequency ratio of seven octaves is

$$(\tfrac{2}{1})^{7} = 128.$$

That is, over a matter of seven octaves—as, as I mentioned earlier, the difference shows up over smaller intervals—the Pythagorean scale produced a distinct discord. This "discord ratio"—

$$129.75 : 128$$

—is called the "comma of Pythagoras." It is probably fortunate for his reputation that his name is also associated with that right-triangle relationship, since his "comma" caused so much grief over the centuries.

(In fact, that comma may have been Pythagoras's real hang-up, rather than the irrational numbers. But, since Greek music was written for a very limited range, the clash was not noticeable, or, possibly, this is why Greek music was written for such a limited range. In any event, the discrepancy did restrict composers of a much later era, who did want to use a wide range of notes.)

The problem was finally resolved through distributing the comma of Pythagoras over twelve intervals of the scale. The result is called the "equal temperament scale."

The equal temperament scale was proposed at least as early as 1482 by Bartolo Rames, a Spaniard. (Though Arixtoxenus may have had the idea some 2,000 years earlier.) Mersenne correctly calculated the related frequencies and published them in 1636. You would naturally expect that such an innovation would be greeted with a round of cheers from musicians and builders of instruments. But, as with the metric system/British "system" measurements debate, many people had reasons for resisting the change; and as long as two centuries after Mersenne wrote, English organs, for example, were not tuned to equal temperament.

Johann Sebastian Bach had made strong efforts on behalf of equal temperament. His clavichord and harpsichord were tuned to it, and his compositions for these instruments use a wide range of notes. By contrast, his organ works are much more restricted.

Finally, with acceptance of the equal temperament scale and the standardization of the pitch of *a,* the following set of frequencies can be arrived at:

c	261.6	f	349.2	a	440
c♯	277.2	f♯	370.0	a♯	466.2
d	293.7	g	392.0	b	493.8
d♯	311.1	g♯	415.3	c′	523.2.
e	329.6				

The easiest arithmetic relationship in this table is that between the frequency of c and that of c♯. If you are inclined to apply a little more arithmetic to this set of frequencies, you will see that there is an increase in frequencies of about 6 per cent from that of c to c♯. That is, multiply the frequency of c by 1.06, and you come very close to the frequency of c♯. Multiply the frequency of c♯ by 1.06, and the result is very close to the frequency of d, and so on. (The actual factor is closer to 1.05946—just in case you are a stickler for accuracy and have a machine for multiplying decimals.)

I'm not really suggesting that you do a great deal of multiplying decimals, but you may want to test one or two cases, just to convince yourself that what I'm saying makes arithmetic sense at least. This number, 1.05946, is a reasonably close approximation to the twelfth root of 2. That is,

$$\sqrt[12]{2} \approx 1.05946.$$

And all this per cent/decimal business is just a way of showing that the 2 : 1 frequency ratio of c′ to c is distributed evenly over the 12 semitones between them.

The following table may help, but if it looks too formidable, skip over it and come back some time when you are feeling more courageous about tackling a batch of numbers:

With c=1, then

c♯≈1.05946	g $\approx (1.05946)^7 \approx 1.4983$
d $\approx (1.05946)^2 \approx 1.1225$	g♯$\approx (1.05946)^8 \approx 1.5874$
d♯$\approx (1.05946)^3 \approx 1.1892$	a $\approx (1.05946)^9 \approx 1.6818$
e $\approx (1.05946)^4 \approx 1.2599$	a♯$\approx (1.05946)^{10} \approx 1.7818$
f $\approx (1.05946)^5 \approx 1.3348$	b $\approx (1.05946)^{11} \approx 1.8878$
f♯$\approx (1.05946)^6 \approx 1.4142$	c′ $\approx (1.05946)^{12} \approx 2.0000$.

(And you can check the multiplication, if you like. There is one thing you can be sure of. After typing this manuscript, I know the twelfth root of 2, to five decimal places—one of the least often asked questions in the world today. You might note, in this table, the ratios of the fifth and fourth, for example, compared to the Pythagorean ratios.)

Since all of these frequency ratios are, after all, approximations, every pitch is just a bit out of tune. A solution to this problem, or at least a way to improve the situation, is to increase the number of subdivisions of the scale. In fact, a 53-note scale was proposed at least as early as the mid-sixteenth century by Gerardus Mercator. There are obvious advantages in regard to mere humans playing such scales, but, possibly, with the coming of computer-generated and electronically produced music, such a scale will become a practicality.

A tuning fork does indeed produce a monotonous sound. And the corresponding curve is equally monotonous. But if you combine tones, you get more interesting sounds and correspondingly more interesting curves. For example, if you combine these two curves

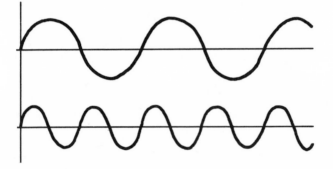

representing tones of two different frequencies, you get something that looks like this:

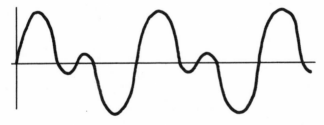

(Nancy Linn.)

Of course, the tuning-fork/moving-paper approach is of little help here, but a mathematical analysis of these more complicated curves is possible. Mathematicians attacked the problem, and, in particular, J. B. J. Fourier showed that any such curves can be broken down into simple curves. The implications are rather startling, to say the least, and Sir James Jeans proposes a dramatic illustration:

"Before a symphony can be played by an orchestra, there must be collaboration of many parties—a composer, the makers and the players of many instruments, and the conductor of the orchestra. All are, or have been, at work to produce—just a curve. If they have done their work well, the sound that this curve represents will be both pleasing to our ears and interesting to our minds. The composer, in writing his score, has given a first rough indication of the curve he desires—he has, so to speak, specified its main ingredients and the instants at which they are to join the general mêlée. It is the business of the instrument-maker and the players to see that these ingredients are of good quality, while the function of the conductor is to see that they join in at the right moments and in the right proportions. All the art, all the mannerisms, all the successes and failures of these many workers are embodied in the one single curve. This curve *is* the symphony—neither more nor less, and the symphony will sound noble or tawdry, musical or harsh, refined or vulgar, according to the quality of this curve."

If the sound produced by a symphony orchestra can be dissected and analyzed, why not consider the possibility of producing the same sound, without involving an orchestra? Seem a little "far out"?

Fourier probably couldn't have imagined such a possibility. And, even at the time Jeans wrote (the first edition of *Science and Music* appeared in 1937), the idea of synthetic orchestra music was, at best, a remote possibility—a possibility which Sir James recognized, by the way. Modern technology has risen to the challenge, however, and, whether or not you like the idea, electronic music is with us.

Electronic music is one important component of the modern "fine arts." In this, mathematics plays a significant part.

Electronic music is the future.

GLENN GOULD

I have always had barely hidden doubts about much of contemporary music. I understand abstract music. I know what composers are trying to do; I have myself written quite a lot of abstract music but always I have had a sense of unease. Now I see why. Abstract music represents an attempt by very highly skilled people to eliminate from music the essential component which they themselves lack, the emotional fires. Abstract music is an attempt to make technique sufficient, an indefensible position, I think. For why on this basis should one not be a mathematician? Music is the wrong profession for the purely abstract.

FRED HOYLE

Math in Mod

If the problem of synthetic generation of music sounds was merely that of reproducing the pure tones of the tuning forks mentioned in an earlier chapter, there would be little challenge for musician, mathematician, and electronics engineer alike. But, for a beginning, the sounds produced by musical instruments are all very complex combinations of tones and overtones—resonances and harmonics.

At that, the mathematical tool for achieving such analysis and synthesis has been available for some time. It was provided, basically, by the work of the French mathematician, Jean Baptiste Joseph Fourier, who lived during the last decades of the eighteenth and first of the nineteenth centuries. Fourier's analysis is rather mathematically "old hat" these days but, back a few years, was considered a worthy subject for Ph.D. dissertations; so a thorough discussion is hardly appropriate here, even were I mathematically capable of providing such. However, an example may give you an idea of what is involved.

Suppose you were to try to duplicate a sound which shows up graphically as a triangular wave, like this:

You can generate tones, and harmonics, which show up graphically as sine waves, of the same kind as those produced by the tuning forks. For example, you could have waves like these:

(Nancy Linn.)

Now, combine the tones, graphically, to get something like this

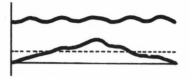

(Nancy Linn.)

—an adequate approximation to the original graph, and a reasonable basis for the synthesis of the original sound.

This kind of graphic illustration is particularly appropriate, since it corresponds to the cathode-ray oscilloscope pictures of sounds. The oscilloscope is often used in the analysis and synthesis of musical sounds because it is more generally available than are the more sophisticated band analyzers.

Once you have what you consider an adequate reconstruction of the musical sound, how do you go about reproducing it? Here, modern technology is providing a remarkable variety of devices, and the fight, as they say, has only yet begun.

Actually, my last statement is technically not accurate, since the first rotary-magnetic sound generator was designed by C. H. Page in 1837. He had all the necessary theory but lacked the technology to apply his theory. (I can't help but compare Page's predicament to that of the better-known Charles Babbage, who, about the same time, designed a digital computer remarkably similar to prototypes of the 1940s. Babbage, also, was frustrated by the inadequacies of the technology of his time.)

Thaddeus Cahill built the first complex tone generator in 1897, but it is only within the last few years that technicians and engineers have begun to produce instruments—vibrating reed generators, vibrating string generators, electromagnetic tuning-fork systems and a substantial variety of sophisticated electrostatic generators which begin to do justice to the theory.

A prediction is that the electromagnetic tuning-fork system will be best used in the generation of new tones, rather than in synthesis of conventional tones. This observation seems, to me, a good lead-in to the question of evaluation and acceptance of the kinds of sounds that come out of "synthetic musical instruments." All mathematics and technology aside, you come to the moment of truth—how does your audience react to electronic music?

There are elements which cannot be accounted for by mathematical theory. While the frequency of A, let's say, can be regulated by international agreement, and the harmonics analyzed, there is still the consideration of timbre or quality of the tone, which varies with the instrument. The assessment of pitch is subjective, and even if every person did hear the same range of tones, the mathematician would be hard put to describe what goes on. Electronic tones have been described as "too smooth." They lack the "noise" which we have come to associate, consciously or unconsciously, with conventional instruments—the plucking noise associated with the playing of the bass viol or harp, the wind escaping in reed instruments, the scraping of the hair of the bow on the violin. And there are "starting noises" associated with many wind instruments, including the organ. An excess of such noise would be a distraction, but those minimal noises which are always present we have come to accept. And when they do not appear in electronic music, the hearer is inclined to say, at best sometimes, "It's certainly different."

There is the even more elusive quality, mentioned by Mr. Hoyle—the "emotional fires,"—or "richness" of tone. I suspect we will not be building that into the electronic systems nor reducing it to mathematical analysis, at least, not for some time yet.

Electronic music is still in its infancy and suffers because, as an infant, it is imitative. Comparison with what has been accepted for many years is bound to produce much adverse reaction. But even now, musicians are experimenting with new sounds, and I believe it will be only a matter of time before these new sounds are accepted. There is no real analog in the history of music—the change is too dramatic. But this seems only in keeping with dramatic changes in all facets of contemporary society.

Symbolic of the dramatic change is the computer. And the computer may provide answers to some of the problems confronting experimenters in electronic music. Serious experimentation in computer-generated music has been going on at such universities as Princeton, MIT, and Yale, some of it supported by the National Science Foundation, and at the Argonne National Laboratory.

Information theory, a new branch of mathematics, "invented" in 1948 by C. E. Shannon, provides a basis for computer-generated music. Any sound can be described in terms of numbers—quite a few numbers for complex sounds, but still a finite array. In fact, 20,000 three-digit numbers a second can describe any music that has been or can be written. Digital computers produce numbers, and fairly quickly at that. Theoretically, the real problem is just that of choosing the right numbers.

I say "theoretically," since, right now, even very fast computers take several seconds to produce enough numbers to describe one sound of music. With computer time going at several hundred dollars an hour, practical generation of music by computer appears to be well in the future.

On the other hand, the speed of computers has been increasing at a remarkable pace. And recent technological breakthroughs promise substantial cost reductions. If these "hardware" improvements materialize, the use of computers in the production of music will be limited only by the imagination, intuition, and experience of the programmers.

Dr. J. R. Pierce, writing in *New Scientist* (February 18, 1965), describes the user of the computer as presently being "in somewhat the position of a musically talented savage when confronted with a grand piano. Certainly, wonderful things can come out of the box, but how is one to bring this about? Tuition, intuition, and practice are required, but there is no teacher and no one to guide the practice."

This is an area in which the computer specialist, talented musician, and the person who understands psychoacoustics can, and must, co-operate—a chance for fruitful co-operation between science and the arts, rather than "the phoney invocation of scientific formulae and jargon which so often satisfies artists in the present."

From such experimentation, both science and the arts will benefit.

The form, then, is that part of the world which we decide to shape, while leaving the rest of the world where it is. The context is that part of the world which puts demands on this form. . . . The form is the solution to the problem; the context defines the problem."

CHRISTOPHER ALEXANDER

It is one thing for the ancient Greeks to build their elaborate temples, with or without the "golden rectangle." Such architecture must be an art form. But what about architecture that would serve the people of the time? Is that an art form? Is the question worth considering? Or, can you argue that, at the time, homage to the gods was a service to the people?

And, again, it was all very well for the seventeenth-century architect to design "the ideal villa," with aesthetically desirable proportions. But how did it work out as a place to live? And since I suspect that not everyone of the time lived in a villa, what could the architect offer the others?

Wait a minute. . . .

Are these legitimate concerns of the artist-architect?

Are these legitimate concerns of the mathematician?

I'll load up the question a bit and try to put it in what I consider appropriate context.

Is this question of whether or not the design of a building reflects the needs of ordinary people a responsibility of the artist?

Is it a responsibility of the mathematician?

And . . . before you say it . . . is this a legitimate concern of someone who attempts to write on "mathematics and the fine arts"? (You aren't necessarily stuck with it. You can always close it up.)

I'll cite a "for instance."

Professor Christopher Alexander, whom I have just quoted, is an English mathematician working at the University of California. He has focused his attention upon the problem of designing buildings—particularly multiple-unit housing complexes (condominiums, if you will)—that truly serve the needs of people in an urban society. Dr. Alexander talks in terms of "cultural anthropology," which seems far removed from both "fine arts" and "mathematics." But he also says such things as "The ultimate object of design is form . . . pattern," which smacks of both art and mathematics.

And, appropriately for our time, Alexander and others, who have addressed themselves to this problem, have made extensive use of the computer in this "decision-making theory." They begin by listing considerations which affect the design and form of such buildings. I'll list a few to give you an idea of the complexity of the problem:

([A new complex should not block natural light from the surrounding areas.
([Owners should be able to be independent and uncrowded, or group together and interact socially whenever they desire
([A dwelling unit should be effectively isolated from disturbing noises from outside the unit boundaries.
([Automobiles need to be located in space that cannot be occupied more efficiently or economically by some other use.
([Utilities need to be easily accessible for repairs, additions, alterations, etc., but should not be visual or physical obstacles.
([An owner should have substantial control of the interior physicial characteristics of his unit without affecting other owners and units.

And so it goes for 72 "requirements." All 72 are related to each other, however remotely, and the ideal would be to maximize realization of all characteristics. The complexity of this undertaking would stump a computer, much less a human architect-sociologist, so the mathematicians working on the problem broke the set of 72 into 13 subsets (not necessarily disjoint) consisting of requirements which seemed to be most closely related. They then established a graph of the relationships among the 13 subsets and tried for optimum realization of the requirements.

There is practically no mention of considerations of beauty in the list of 72, but perhaps "utility" is a fitting and appropriate characteristic of the twentieth-century partnership of mathematics and architecture.

California Computer Products sponsored a computer art contest to "humanize computer-plotter technology—to show that art forms can be created and developed to dramatize aesthetic values, along with materialistic uses." These are the three top winners.

11. "Cross," by Gordon Hines of Queens University, Kingston.

12. "Tancentric," by Mrs. Linda Sue Lowery, who works as a research programmer analyst at George Washington University and is an evening school student in painting.

13. "Oscillating
Wastebasket," by
George Olshevsky, Jr.,
of Buffalo, New York.

By keenly confronting the enigmas that surround us, and by considering and analyzing the observations that I had made, I ended
up in the realm of mathematics. Although I am absolutely inno-
cent of training or knowledge in the exact sciences, I often seem
to have more in common with mathematicians than with my fellow artists.

M. C. ESCHER

Artists worked for several hundred years to arrive at a scientific
prescription for perspective, and then along comes M. C. Escher
and deliberately demolishes the whole business.

14. "Waterfall," by M. C. Escher. (With permission of the Escher Association.)

15. "Relativity," by M. C. Escher. (With permission of the Escher Association.)

Ordinarily, I am inclined to let an illustration stand on its own. But Escher's works seem to need a little interpretation; at least, I managed to miss many of the features until I read the artist's remarks. So, here is M. C. Escher describing "Relativity," a lithograph by M. C. Escher—and you can "do" the others yourself.

"Here we have three forces of gravity working perpendicularly to one another. Three earth-planes cut across each other at right-angles, and human beings are living on each of them. It is im-

If Escher's distortions of perspective seem a bit difficult to emulate, try your hand at one or another of these. (Nancy Linn.)

possible for the inhabitants of different worlds to walk or sit or stand on the same floor, because they have differing conceptions of what is horizontal and what is vertical. Yet they may well share the use of the same staircase. On the top staircase illustrated here, two people are moving side by side and in the same direction, and yet one of them is going downstairs and the other upstairs. Contact between them is out of the question, because they live in different worlds and therefore can have no knowledge of each other's existence."

Incidentally, Escher not only has taken extreme liberties with perspective, but he would challenge such a revered maxim as "A picture is worth a thousand words." Listen to this: "It is a fact that most people find it easier to arrive at an understanding of an image by the roundabout method of letter symbols than by the direct route."

Well, there you have a sampling of modern interpretations in the fine arts—computer music, computer art, utilitarian architecture, M. C. Escher. The variety and extent of what has been done, and is being tried, defy description and imagination, but, possibly out of these experiments will come an answer to the challenge that Claude Bragdon proposed in 1927:

"The modern mind has adventured far and fearlessly in the new realms of thought opened up by research and discovery, but it has left no trail of beauty. That it has not done so is the fault of the artist, who has failed to interpret and portray the movement of the modern mind. . . . The new beauty, which corresponds to the new knowledge, is the beauty of principles . . . the world order. The world order is most perfectly embodied in mathematics."

A picture is worth a thousand words.

Modern (?) proverb

It is a fact, that most people find it easier to arrive at an understanding of an image by the roundabout method of letter symbols than by the direct route.

M. C. Escher

Math Forms in Art

M. C. Escher to the contrary, I'll include here a few examples of "pure" (or, almost pure) math forms in artistic contexts with minimum commentary.

The engravings of Wendel Dietterlin reflect the secular spirit of the seventeenth century, though not all were as mathematical in form as this. "This was not only the time of the Reformation and Counter Reformation, but also the time of vast scientific discoveries, the time of Copernicus, Galileo, and Kepler. It was also a time of alchemy and phantasy."

A bit op-artish, perhaps, but it does give an interesting effect (I think), and it's one you can do yourself.

Mark off the circumference of the circle into 30 equal parts. (I stepped off the radius around the circle, giving six equal parts, and then divided each of those into five small parts.) Number the marks from 1 to 30. Join a point with that point whose number is fifteen times that of the first point, reduced modulus 31.

For example, if the point is numbered 5, you multiply $5 \times 15 = 75$, and take the remainder when 75 is divided by 31 . . . that is, 13. Join point 5 with point 13 and proceed around the circle.

Then black in alternate areas.

Or maybe you prefer to blacken the hexagons.

The cuboctahedron is one of the thirteen semiregular, which are sometimes called "Archimedean." Faces of the cuboctahedron are equilateral triangles and squares. Cut off just the proper piece from each corner of a cube, and you have a cuboctahedron. Cut

Engraving by Wendel Dietterlin. (From THE FANTASTIC ENGRAVINGS OF WENDEL DIETTERLIN. With permission of Dover Publications.)

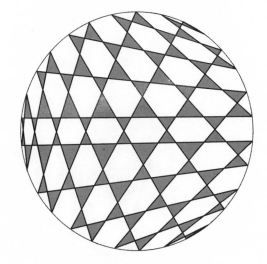

Design based on a
circle marked off in
equal intervals and
points joined
according to a
modulus 31 system.
(Nancy Linn.)

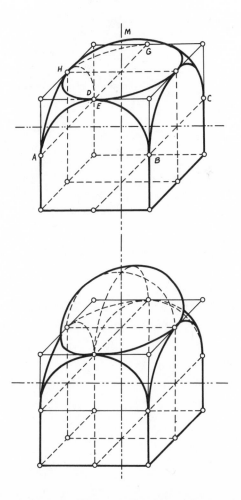

Byzantine cupolas,
based on the
cuboctahedron.

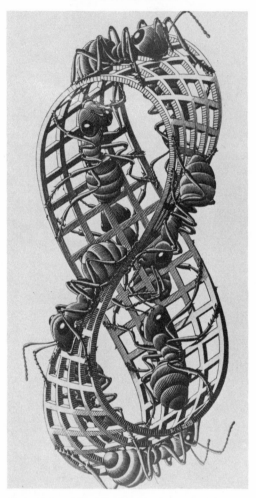

16. "Möbius Strip," by Maurits C. Escher. (With permission of the Escher Association.)

off just the right amount from each corner of a regular octahedron and you have . . . that's right, a cuboctahedron.

But make your cuts rounded and add a hemisphere and you have a Byzantine cupola.

The Möbius strip has caught the fancy of quite a few people these days. In case you haven't run into it (or over it), the idea is

The artist-programmer first fed into the computer the mathematical formulas for the desired designs. The computer digested the information, performed a few thousand calculations, and then sent instructions to the mechanical plotter which actually drew the designs.

17, 18. Two more Rutherford Boyd studies in artistic effects obtained from mathematical forms. (Rutherford Boyd photo, from SCRIPTA MATHEMATICA, and with the permission of the Rutherford Boyd Estate.)

19. Begin with a polygon and some judiciously placed points. Join with straight lines only, and this is a result. (Jeff Linn.)

that it is a one-sided surface—it can be traversed completely with any edges being crossed. Here Escher has the ants doing the traversing. You can trace their progress and prospects.

This sampling would not be complete without a couple of Rutherford Boyd math-art forms.

The possibilities are unbounded for the development of the mathematics-fine-arts theme, but I believe I'll rest my introduction at this point, and leave the follow-up to you. May be that you have now heard more than you really wanted to hear about mathematics and the fine arts. In which case, you may want to consider such an alternative as "mathematics in (and through) literature and poetry."

Or, if the fine-arts theme appeals, you could go from here to some of the books mentioned in the Bibliography. But, I urge you, rather, to try out some of these ideas yourself. Have you actually tried sketches incorporating the rules of perspective? Have you examined the varieties of repeated design and tried creating some yourself? Or, if you have access to a computer, you might try some computer art. If Escher's work appeals, have a go at some distortions of perspective, or imaginative blendings of symmetry.

Neither mathematics nor art is a spectator sport.

APPENDIX

A Cast of Characters

Leon Battista Alberti was much intrigued with the properties of number, though his reputation rests upon his study of perspective and of proportion, about which he wrote quite a bit. He designed a number of churches, did some painting, and played the organ—in the early fifteenth century.

Archibald Alison was a Scot and an Episcopal clergyman, who lived in the eighteenth century. His book of essays entitled, simply enough, *Taste,* was much admired in his time. His grandson and namesake was an army general who wrote a best seller called *On Army Organization.*

Thomas Aquinas. A "system of thought" called "Scholasticism" developed in the thirteenth and fourteenth centuries. Thomas Aquinas was one of the more articulate Scholastics. This was a very logical—I would say "sterile"—business, and the Scholastics seemed to get terribly hung-up on points which the average citizen regarded as slightly ridiculous. (I am not sure that the Scholastics did debate the question: "How many angels can you get on the head of a pin?" But I've found very close approximations in the writings of Aquinas.)

Aristoxenus lived some years after the Pythagorean music theory was well established, and he became distressed at the idea that "the cogitations of theorists"—particularly, mathematical theorists—should receive more attention than the observations of the musicians.

Charles Babbage lived a hundred years too soon. He had all the ideas for a digital computer, but no one could build the parts to the needed degree of precision. So, he blew quite a bit of the taxpayers' money, back in the 1840s, and didn't have much to show for it. The story is that he also devised a sure-fire scheme for winning at betting on horses.

Johann Sebastian Bach was evidently more public spirited than was Beethoven, since there is no record of the latter's agitating for equal-temperament scale. But maybe that fight was already won by Beethoven's time. On the other hand, if Bach's reputation had rested on that bit of reform, you might never have heard of him.

J. Murray Barbour's *Tuning and Temperament, A Historical Survey* must be the definitive work on that subject. If you need to be convinced that there's much math in music theory, take a look at this book. Mr. Barbour has also written articles on math and music which have appeared in *Scripta Mathematica,* among other places.

Ludwig van Beethoven's name used to be almost synonymous with "music," though some people will argue that I really mean Bach, or Brahms, or the Beatles. Anyway, he did very well at it, and apparently J. Murray Barbour thinks so, since he cites a Beethoven composition along with a Michelangelo creation as the ultimate challenges for the person who would establish mathematical criteria for the arts.

Boethius is called "the last of the noble Romans." He lived in the sixth century, after Rome had been conquered by the people from the north. His writings have helped considerably in preserving some of the ancient Greek mathematics. Boethius was a pagan, but somehow has become known as a Christian martyr. He was indeed eliminated by one of the Visigoth rulers.

Rutherford Boyd devoted much time over a period of thirty years investigating the relationship between mathematics and art.

He experimented with many models, and his photos of some of these, which are sprinkled around this book, appeared originally in *Scripta Mathematica*. He also produced a math-art film called *Parabola*.

Claude Bragdon was an architect who was particularly interested in stage design and four-dimensional space. His *Projective Ornament* is particularly fascinating. He is also described, somewhere, as a "theosophist." I had to look that up.

Michelangelo Buonarroti. Many people do not know that this Buonarroti fellow wrote many sonnets, love poems, and madrigals, as well as some philosophic poems. He was also one of nine citizens charged with the defense of Florence in 1529. He seems to have survived a goodly number of changes in popes, for whom he worked—and now his name is almost universally synonymous with "art"—but how many of those popes can you name? I recommend Irving Stone's biographical novel of Michelangelo, *The Agony and the Ecstasy*.

Jacob Burckhardt was a professor of history at Basel University, particularly interested in the history of art. His study, *The Civilization of the Renaissance in Italy* (1860), has become almost a classic.

Edmund Burke's is one of the great names in the history of political literature, but, since his name appears here, 'tis obvious that he did not confine his commentaries to matters political. He spoke well of the rebels in that disagreement the English Government was having with some folks in North America.

Thaddeus Cahill lived half his life in the nineteenth century and half in the twentieth. He invented an electric typewriter and also a device for producing music at distant points by means of alternating currents of electricity, controlled by an operator who plays on a keyboard.

Cardan—sometimes, Cardano—had a first name of Jerome, but very few people these days mention that. Some say he was a great mathematician, and others argue that he was one of the great rascals of his time. (And there were more than a few rascals in the sixteenth century.) He was a physician, also, and wrote on matters of the anatomy and probability. You may want to read Oystein Ore's biography, *Cardan, the Gambling Scholar.*

Samuel Taylor Coleridge wrote once to his brother deploring the lack of imagination on the part of those who participate in mathematics: "Reason is feasted, while imagination is starved." I can't agree with him, but, on the other hand, many math types certainly give this impression. Coleridge also wrote *The Ancient Mariner,* and the recently published annotated edition is annotated by a mathematician—Martin Gardner.

Salvador Dali completed two portraits, one of Helen of Troy, before he was ten years old. (I don't think he did that portrait from life.) He also designed a "dream house" for the 1939 New York World's Fair and wrote *Diary of a Genius.*

René Descartes was one of the few mathematicians who had a fairly serious voluntary go at soldiering. He is also reported to have been addicted to sleeping very late—in fact, spending much of the time in bed. Mathematically, he is best remembered for the "Cartesian" co-ordinates, which he didn't really invent. His philosophy was well thought of at one time or another.

Albrecht Dürer was a sixteenth-century German painter and engraver, but he was much more than that. He applied a scientific approach to the theory of proportion and did some interesting and important work in perspective. He even tried his hand at writing poetry, which, so the story goes, he asked some friends to read and criticize. They laughed at him, whereupon he responded with a poem called *Good and Bad Friends.* He also wrote a geometry text, intended for the young and "for those who have had no one to instruct them accurately." Dürer evidently had a sense of humor too; read, sometime, his directions to someone who wished to place a monument over the grave of a drunkard.

Maurits C. Escher says that he actually "sees" those scenes as "visual images" before he begins to work on them. You really should get hold of the book—which is what I did—and read Escher's descriptions of his artistic efforts. Wild, but subtle, and it may be that, 100 years or so from now, the "authorities" will say that Escher best represented his time.

Euclid collected the mathematical results up to his time (fourth century B.C.) in the *Elements,* a monumental work. The geometry part of his *Elements* is still essentially the basis for the study of geometry in high schools. Euclid was one of the first to work at the library in Alexandria, established as a center of study by Ptolemy, one of the lieutenants of Alexander the Great.

Leonhard Euler. Even in an era of great mathematicians—the eighteenth century—Euler stood out. He is regarded as one of the founders of "pure" mathematics, but he also did some serious work in optics, astronomy, and other applied areas, including the invention of a system of logarithms based on the musical scale. (His name, incidentally, is pronounced "Oiler"—which prompted a friend of mine to ask, "If Euler is 'Oiler,' why isn't Euclid, 'Oiclid'?" No one seems sure.)

Fibonacci. Since "Fibonacci" really means "son of the simpleton," according to some translations, you may want to call him "Leonardo of Pisa." He made quite a reputation for himself among his thirteenth-century contemporaries, by beating everyone around in math contests. His current fame seems to rest upon the versatility of that sequence I mentioned. The sequence, so the story goes, came from an attempt by Fibonacci to count the descendants of a pair of bunnies.

J. B. J. Fourier was one of the few mathematicians who made a go at politics. He accompanied Napoleon Bonaparte to Egypt, and wound up as governor of half of that country. His political fortunes fluctuated with Bonaparte's, but he did hold offices in France later. J.B.J. should not be confused with F. C. M. Fourier, who lived about the same time, had, as you will notice, the same number of initials, and advocated a rather extreme form of socialism.

Piero della Francesca died in the year Columbus made his first trip to the West Indies, but he has become more popular recently, "due," one authority says, "to the mathematical perfection of his forms and to his superb sense of interval."

Glenn Gould is an outstanding, young contemporary pianist, who bailed out of the concert circuit and has been devoting himself to recordings and television productions. I guess you might call his music "straight," but he seems to have a good sense of what is going on in the way of technological innovations that affect the production and consumption of music. I find his remarks on concerts most refreshing.

Jay Hambidge, who lived through a quarter of this century, was committed to the idea that the Greeks designed their temples around the "golden section" and other irrational numbers. In fact, he even wrote books on the business, which he called "dynamic symmetry." Whether or not you buy his arguments, there's much good and interesting geometry in those books.

Hermann Ludwig Ferdinand von Helmholtz—but his list of significant contributions to a variety of sciences is much longer even than his name. He was one of the founders of the theory of conservation of energy, did important studies in electricity and nerve impulses, and his *Sensations of Tone* is considered a classic work.

Frans Hemsterhuis was an eighteenth-century Dutch philosopher. He is described in one source as "leaning toward an aesthetic, pantheistic Neoplatonism." I guess this means, among other things, that he believed that everything you see provides evidence of some unifying force or spirit throughout the universe.

Villard de Honnecourt. Not much more is known about him than what I've said already. Apparently he traveled in Hungary, and it may be that he sketched the sketches in his sketchbook to take along and show the folks he met in his travels.

Fred Hoyle writes good science fiction—at least, I enjoy his books. He is also a Fellow of the Royal Society on the basis of his outstanding work in astronomy, astrophysics, and mathematics. If the science fiction doesn't interest you, try *The Nature of the Universe* or *Frontiers of Astronomy*.

Sir James Jeans. The "Sir" seems to come naturally, which is why I used it here. Sir James was doing very well as a mathematician when he gave it up and turned to writing popularizations of science. Tallulah Bankhead recommended his *The Mysterious Universe* as a book that every girl should read. Jeans was also a very capable organist, so his *Science and Music* is based on more than mere theory.

Lord Kames was known familiarly as Henry Home. He gained a reputation in eighteenth-century Scotland as a judge and philosopher on the basis of writing such things as *Essays on the Principles of Morality and Natural Religion*.

Immanuel Kant's name is usually recognized, although I'm not sure how many people can say what he stood for. Anyway, he is best known as a philosopher, but he also lectured early in his career on matters scientific and mathematic and once refused a professorship of poetry. He had a low opinion of women and never married.

Jean Etienne Liotard lived through most of the eighteenth century, which was quite an accomplishment, considering the state of the medical profession and the lack of indoor plumbing in France. He painted mostly "graceful and delicate pastels" and was popularly known as "that Turkish painter" because he was given to wearing exotic oriental costumes.

Henry Wadsworth Longfellow:

> Under a spreading chestnut-tree
> The village smithy stands, . . .

and,   By the shore of Gitche Gumee,
          By the shining Big-Sea-Water, . . .

Need I say more?

Marshall McLuhan's name is, I'm told, almost a household word these days. He has, among other things, attempted to assess the impact of modern communications media, particularly television, on the young people of our time. Some of his writings are tough enough reading to convince you that he is right in saying that books are obsolete. But his *The Medium Is the Massage* is quite a remarkable integration of graphic and written presentation and makes me think that what is needed is just a different kind of book.

Gerhardus Mercator is the same chap for whom the Mercator map projection is named. He was principally a geographer, and a sixteenth-century Flemish geographer at that, and should not be confused with a seventeenth-century German mathematician and engineer, Nicholas Mercator, whose real name was Kaufmann.

Marin Mersenne was born in the year of the Spanish Armada, which made him a contemporary of some of the great mathematicians —Fermat, Pascal, Descartes—and he served as the latter's agent in Paris while Descartes was languishing in exile in Holland. Mersenne wrote *The Universal Harmony,* and numbers of the form $2^p - 1$, where p is a prime, are still called "Mersenne numbers."

David Middleton was a student of G. D. Birkhoff's at Harvard, and more than that I've been unable to find. But that cat's face is a rather remarkable business.

Francisco Pacheco, a Spanish painter and art historian, ran a very popular art academy in the early seventeenth century. Some of his best paintings are located in two churches at Alcalá de Guadaira, and you might take a look the next time you are down that way.

Plato is usually described as a philosopher, but he dabbled more than somewhat in mathematics and commented on most everything, including the arts. In mathematics he started some things—such as the rule about using only compass and straightedge for constructions—which took people quite a few centuries to finish. Plato's original name was Aristocles, but hardly anyone called him that.

Pliny the Elder is best remembered for his *Natural History* which was truly an encyclopaedic work. He also wrote a paper entitled "On Throwing the Javelin from Horseback, in One Book," while he was commander of a Roman cavalry regiment. He was killed in the great eruption of Mount Vesuvius, and you really should read the dramatic story of his demise.

Plotinus is said to have lived in the third century, but things were in such a state of turmoil then and afterward that I doubt that anyone can be sure. Anyway, he is said to have studied in Alexandria, Egypt, where so many scholars congregated in those days. He is further said to have been of Roman parentage which fits in nicely with my theory about Roman mathematicians and such. He was also a leading spokesman for Neoplatonic philosophy, but you'll have to look that up, since I'm not at all sure I understand it myself.

Edgar Allan Poe was one of my favorite people long before I found that he was somewhat addicted to mathematics. His mystery tales, "The Gold Bug," for example, and his horror stories, such as *The Fall of the House of Usher*, aren't as wild and horrible as are some of the contemporary efforts, but maybe that's not so bad. I wonder if you could combine Poe's poetry and Escher's woodcuts and lithographs into a mood book for math types?

Marcus Vitruvius Pollio seems to have been shorn of both first and
last names, since it is as "Vitruvius" that he is remembered as
the great writer on Greek and Roman architecture. His style
was confusing, and misinterpretations have produced some
really startling results. (Check, sometime, on the bronze vase
muddle.)

Georges Polya is one of those rare individuals who is both a great
mathematician and a great teacher. If you haven't read any of
his books, I would recommend you begin with *How to Solve
It.* And this goes, whether you are a math type or not.

Claudius Ptolemy is best known as a geographer and as the chap
whose geocentric theory of the solar system was finally de-
molished by Copernicus, seventeen hundred or so years later.
Ptolemy also wrote on music, as did any math-science type
worth his salt, and proposed, as a solution to the Aristoxenus-
Pythagorean argument, that the tuning is best for which the
ear and the mathematical ratio are in agreement. We don't
know how he proposed to accomplish this, but possibly that
was in the portion of his work that was lost.

Pythagoras is a very obscure figure now, to say the least. And there
are even people who suggest that he was not really a single
person, but rather a composite. Nevertheless, his is one of the
best-known names in elementary mathematics, since it is associated with that business of the "square on the hypotenuse"
of a right triangle. Some of the ideas of the mystic brotherhood,
which he is supposed to have founded, are still referred to by
present-day Masonic lodges.

Claude E. Shannon, with Warren Weaver, launched information
theory in the late forties. You might be interested in reading his
article on a "Chess-playing Machine" in Newman's *World of
Mathematics.*

David Eugene Smith was an outstanding teacher of mathematics—
most often associated with Columbia University—whose principal interest was in the history of the subject. His two-volume

History, I find, always has at least a reference to an incident or person in mathematics up to his time, however obscure, and this, despite the fact, that it was written almost fifty years ago —before a great deal of the scholarship was committed in certain areas.

Herbert Spencer lived almost exactly 100 years after Kant, but since I didn't mention when Kant lived, this wisdom doesn't do you much good. Spencer advocated the pre-eminence of the individual over society, which would put him well out of step these days. He was self-educated, having declined an offer from an uncle to finance his way to Cambridge. As it turned out, the uncle left him a substantial quantity of money anyway.

James Joseph Sylvester's principal field was mathematics, but he also got involved in trying to systematize the writing of poetry. Which seems as good a time as any to recommend E. T. Bell's *Men of Mathematics,* which includes a biographical sketch of Sylvester.

Paolo Uccello was one of the first to give serious attention to the problems of perspective and, according to Vasari, was carried away with the study. He also did some mosaics and stained-glass windows. Like most of the artists of the time, Uccello did work, on commission, for leading religious and civil figures of the time. One such abbott apparently gave him only cheese to eat, which caused him to abandon the job, lest "I be no more Paolo, but cheese."

Giorgio Vasari. Vasari was a painter in his own right, having studied under Michelangelo, but he is best known for his *Lives of the Most Eminent Painters, Sculptors, and Architects* (sometimes called just *Lives*). This book is a chief source of information on the artists from the time of Giotto to that of the author and is full of interesting and humorous anecdotes about the people involved.

Leonardo da Vinci. I had thought that almost everyone agreed that Leonardo (and, you'll sometimes find him listed under "Vinci") was a "universal genius." But, in keeping with the current notion that everyone should be cut down to size, some people are saying that he was a jack-of-all-trades . . . and some less nice things. For my money, he did many things—painting, sculpting, engineering—well. Tried his hand at architecture and proposed some remarkable scientific ideas, including the suggestion that one might build a machine that would fly through the air.

Jan Vredeman de Vries is sometimes referred to as just "Hans." He was known at times as the "Flemish Vitruvius." Probably many people had trouble sorting out his architectural fantasies and grotesques from his serious suggestions; his books are described as "fantasies and textbooks, dreams and pattern-books for apprentices." I think Vitruvius was quite a bit more serious about the entire business.

Christopher Wren designed many buildings to replace those destroyed in the London fire of 1666. His best-known work is St. Paul's Cathedral. He also proposed a new plan for London, which had wide avenues radiating from a central space. If you have been to London, you will realize that he lost that argument. Sir Christopher was recognized by none other than Sir Isaac Newton for his work in geometry.

BIBLIOGRAPHY

If this book created a "mood" for mathematics and the fine arts, perhaps some of the following will help you to go a step further. That is, the books and articles listed here are but a small sample of what has been written about the various topics. They are, I believe, rather useful sources and not too difficult.

Music by the Easy Numbers

Archibald, R. C., "Mathematics and Music," *American Mathematical Monthly*, 31:1 (1924).

Barbour, J. M., "The Pythagorean Tuning System," *Scripta Mathematica*, 1:287 (1932).

Barbour, J. M., *Tuning and Temperament, A Historical Survey*, Michigan State University Press, 1951.

Proportions, Divine and Otherwise

Bowie, T., ed., *The Sketchbook of Villard de Honnecourt*, Indiana University Press, 1959.

Dürer, A., *Treatise on Proportions*, Dover, 1917.

Ghyka, M., *Geometry of Art and Life*, Sheed & Ward, 1946.

Gombich, E. H., *Art and Illusion*, Pantheon, 1961.

Scholfield, P. H., *Theory of Proportion in Architecture*, Cambridge University Press, 1958.

Not by Math Alone

Edwards, I. E. S, *The Pyramids of Egypt,* Pelican, 1961.
Petrie, H. M. F., many books, which are old now and out of print, but still seem to be authoritative.

Systematic and Proper Deception

Richter, E., *The Notebooks of Leonardo da Vinci,* Dover, 1970.
Goodyear, W. H., *Greek Refinements,* Yale University Press, 1912.
Jamnitzer, J., *Perspectiva,* 1568.
Vredeman, J., *Perspective,* Dover, 1968.

Symmetry, Patterns, and Ornament

Bragdon, C., *Projective Ornament,* Alfred A. Knopf, 1927.
Audsley, W., and G., *Designs and Patterns From Historic Ornaments,* Dover, 1968.
Weyl, H., *Symmetry,* Princeton University Press, 1952.

The Measure of Beauty

Birkhoff, G. D., *Aesthetic Measure,* Harvard University Press, 1924.
Poe, E. A., "The Rationale of Verse" in any collection of Poe's work.

Curves and Pitch

Coxeter, H. S. M., "Music and Mathematics," *Mathematics Teacher,* National Council of Teachers of Mathematics, March 1968.
Jeans, J., *Science and Music,* Macmillan, 1937.
Miller, D. C., *The Science of Musical Sound,* Macmillan, 1934.

Math in Mod

Douglas, A., *The Electrical Production of Music,* The Philosophical Library, 1957.

Escher, M. C., *The Graphic Works of M. C. Escher,* Meredith, 1967.

Reichardt, J., ed., *Cybernetic Serendipity,* Frederick A. Praeger, 1969.

Math Forms in Art

Baravalle, H., *Geometry in Pictures,* privately published, 1939.

Seymour, D. G., and Schadler, R. A., *Line Designs,* Creative Publications, 1968.

INDEX

A

a, pitch of, 82, 83
Abstract music, 87
Aegina, temple at, 48
Aesthetic Measure (Birkhoff), 66, 71
Agony and the Ecstasy, The (Stone), 111
Alberti, Leon Battista, 15, 109
Alexander, Christopher, 93–94
Alexander the Great, 113
Alhambra, the, 58
Alison, Archibald, 27, 209
Allusions, mathematical illusions and, 1
Ancient Mariner, The (Coleridge), 112
Angles:
  measuring of, 46
  proper appearance of, 39
  of the pyramids, 30
Apollo (deity), 22
Aquinas, Thomas, 15, 109
Arabian diaper ornament, 56
Argonne National Laboratory, 92
Aristotle, 65, 66
Arixtoxenus, 13, 83, 109
Athena (deity), 22

B

Babbage, Charles, 90, 110
Bach, Johann Sebastian, 110
Balance, idea of, 2
Bankhead, Tallulah, 115
Barbour, J. Murray, 63, 110
Beatles, 110
Beauty, measurement of, 65–77
  music, 73–74
  poetry, 74–76
  vase forms, 71–72
Beethoven, Ludwig van, 63, 110
Bell, E. T., 119
Birkhoff, George David, 66, 68–75, 116
Black Death, 26
Boethius, 13, 23, 110
Bonaparte, Napoleon, 114
Boyd, Rutherford, viii, xiv, 105, 106, 110–11
Bragdon, Claude, 53, 60–62, 100, 111
Brahms, Johannes, 110
"Brooklyn Bridge: Variation on an Old Theme, The" (Stella), 5
Burckhardt, Jacob, 46, 111
Burke, Edmund, 15, 66, 111
Byzantine cupolas, 103–6

CHARLES F. LINN lives in Oswego, New York, with his wife, Nancy, who worked with him on this book, and children, Jeff, Jenny, Holly, Heather, and Susan. He teaches at Oswego State College and also teaches a course at Oswego High School. The latter course incorporates many of the geometry-and-art ideas described in this book.

Linn also taught mathematics in Connecticut public schools and was the mathematics editor and writer for two nationally circulated classroom-science newspapers. He has written several books and booklets about mathematics, including two for very young readers, and co-authored a textbook.

The Linns spend their summers in a 180-year-old house on Turkey Hill Road in Haddam, Connecticut, a house they claim to be "rehabilitating on the hundred-year plan."

DATE DUE

MAR 29			
Feb 2			
May 1			
APR 21 978			
MAY 6			
1-31-11			